STEVE PIDD

YOU WILL INDEED BE SET FREE

JOHN 8:36b NLT

Accessing God's promises of Emotional Wholeness, Mental Peace, Spiritual Freedom, Relational Harmony & Physical Wellbeing

ABOUT THE AUTHOR

Steve and his wife Em have spent the majority of their Christian life serving as Senior Pastors in a local Church environment. They have been involved internationally in training and ministering in the areas of healing and freedom for over 20 years. They have developed and conducted their 'School of Healing and Freedom' in various locations in Australia and across the World during that time. In more recent years their ministry abroad has mainly involved teaching and mentoring Pastors and leaders, as well as churches, to be equipped in the areas of healing and freedom ministries. Steve is the founder and International Director of Agape Orphanage Network Australia inc. For information on how to help children in need go to our website. www.aon.org.au

For information regarding locations for Schools in the U.S.A. contact us through our website: www.418centre.org

Copyright
Written and compiled by Steve Pidd
October 2019

All enquiries can be directed in writing to:
Steve Pidd
Email: contact@418centre.org

All rights reserved. This book is copyright. Apart from any fair dealing for the purposes of private study, research, criticism or review, as permitted under the Copyright Act, no part may be reproduced in any form (including electronically) without written permission.

THE HOLY BIBLE, NEW INTERNATIONAL VERSION®, NIV®
Copyright © 1973, 1978, 1984 by Biblica, Inc, ™
Used by permission. All rights reserved worldwide

THE NEW KING JAMES VERSION (NKJV)
Copyright © 1975, 1982 Thomas Nelson Publishers
Used by permission. All rights reserved

HOLY BIBLE, NEW LIVING TRANSLATION®, NLT®
Scripture quotations marked (NLT) are taken from the Holy Bible, New Living Translation, copyright ©1996, 2004, 2015 by Tyndale House Foundation. Used by permission of Tyndale House Publishers, Inc., Carol Stream, Illinois 60188. All rights reserved.

ACKNOWLEDGEMENTS

I want to thank my amazing wife Em who has been my ministry partner throughout the journey that we are on. She is a powerhouse in my life, and has been, and is all of the support that I could ever hope for. I also want to acknowledge our resilient and incredible children Kassie and Daniel. They have patiently endured a seemingly endless stream of people invading their home who were seeking healing and freedom. They have flourished in spite of some of the strange paths that we have taken, I can proudly say, growing into the wonderful adults that they now are.

I would also like to express my gratitude to Professor David Giles and his wife Pauline for all of the hours that have been put into editing this publication.

I would also like to note the generosity of Nigel and Tracey Walters for being instrumental in producing this first edition. They are truly Kingdom minded people.

PREFACE

In this book the author explains the relevance and meaning of the 'heart' from a Biblical perspective. It details how 'truth' ministered to 'heart beliefs' is the basis and key to freedom from issues that have not been able to be resolved through other means, such as anxiety, rejection, inferiority, depression etc.

The publication is an excerpt comprised of the first two sections from the book 'Healing And Freedom Through Truth Encounters.' It has been produced as the result of a growing awareness of the need for a less comprehensive and detailed version of that work.

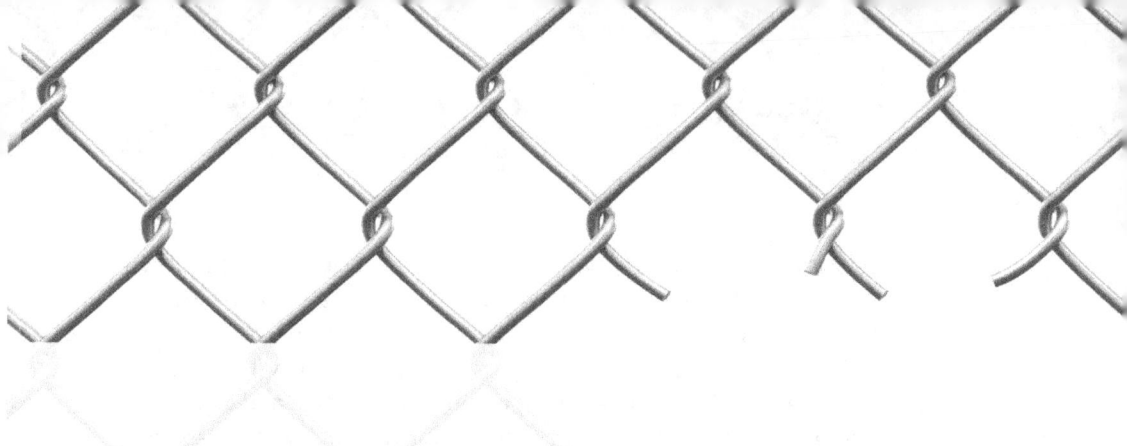

CONTENTS

FOREWORD	8
INTRODUCTION	10

PART 1 - HEALING THROUGH TRUTH FROM A BIBLICAL PERSPECTIVE

Chapter 1: Truth Encounters and 'The Fall of man'	17
Chapter 2: Why grace?	21
Chapter 3: Understanding the biblical meaning of the 'Heart'	27
Chapter 4: The role of memory	33
Chapter 5: Grasshoppers and faith	39
Chapter 6: 'Strongholds' and spiritual warfare	43
Chapter 7: Beliefs produce feelings or what we term emotions	45
Chapter 8: The example of the Apostle Paul's dilemma	49
Chapter 9: Sanctification, healing & freedom come through truth	53
Chapter 10: What is a Broken Heart & who is broken-hearted?	55
Chapter 11: Physical healing through healing the broken heart	59
Chapter 12: Gods own perspective for those suffering in this area	66

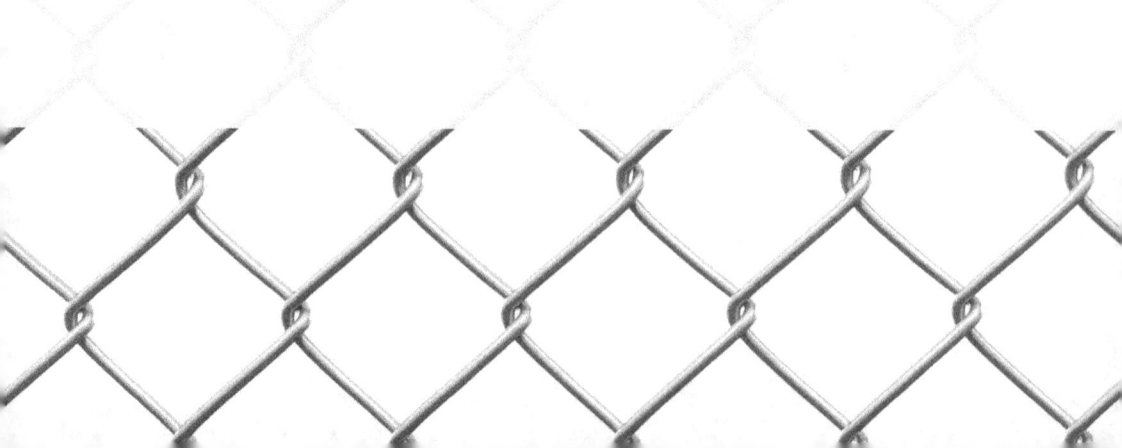

PART 2 - RECEIVING YOUR FREEDOM THROUGH A TRUTH ENCOUNTER
Chapter 13: Accessing the Heart via the mind and emotions   71
Chapter 14: Sources of & Influences on Heart beliefs   79
Chapter 15: Memory   99
Chapter 16: Types of Beliefs   109
Chapter 17: Problem areas that you may periodically encounter   135
Chapter 18: The potential demonic Element   145
Chapter 19: Names of demons and touching the spirit realm   155
Finally   159

Appendix 1 - Centre details and faith statement   160
Appendix 2 - Other Resources   163

FOREWORD

Having attended a great many conferences over the years, my observations are that the modern church is largely concerned with matters such as leadership, growing the numbers in congregations, or church planting. There is no doubt at all that these are wonderful and necessary topics to facilitate the building of the Kingdom of God.

There is, however, very little focus on healing ministries and as a consequence, doctors are the first port of call for physical problems. For many churches, even large city congregations, if there are mental or emotional issues, the people are sent to psychiatrists or Christian counsellors trained in secular techniques.

In contrast if we look at Jesus as the model, His focus was on healing the sick, freeing those with demonic bondages and healing the broken hearted. His disciples freely received this ministry from Christ themselves before they were commissioned to take the World.

*"Heal the sick, raise the dead, cleanse those who have leprosy, drive out demons. Freely **you have received**, freely give"* (NIV, Matthew 10:8, emphasis mine).

Perhaps we could look at it this way. Imagine if you were putting together a football team and selecting your players. "Alright, I choose that man over there with one leg, the blind guy, that deaf fellow, the man with one eye, those chaps with the back braces on, and those cripples." Then you launched them out onto the field, yelling with great enthusiasm and encouragement; "Go get them guys!"

It doesn't make much sense to me but many of us have been around churches where the focus is on trying to motivate broken people to live a victorious life of faith. We have all seen the fallout and problems from people with unresolved issues active in a church environment.

Remember the 'Vasa'
There is an old Swedish warship housed in a museum in Stockholm called by the name of 'Vasa.' She was commissioned to be built by the King of Sweden, Gustavus Adolphus, for use in the war with Poland-Lithuania. The boat was constructed between 1626-27. Upon completion she was considered to be one of the most powerful warships in the world at the time.

A tremendous amount of resources were put into her construction, and she presented with rich and ornate decorations. She was loaded with large and powerful guns. Unfortunately, all of the expense and efforts went into her appearance and equipment for war. Not enough time was spent on the design and what was done below the waterline out of sight. The result was that she appeared to be a splendid, dangerous and formidable enemy, when in fact she was unstable in her foundation and not well ballasted. The guns had just been fired as a grand salute to onlookers as the vessel left Stockholm. Sadly only 1400 meters into her maiden voyage she encountered a gust of wind which caused the ship to capsize and sink.

The lesson seems to be that if we spend all of our time on presentation, and how things look, and neglect dealing with the sub-surface problems of the church, we may not even get into battle. If we train people in leadership and develop or release gifts but don't deal with the unresolved issues in their lives, are we building on sand?

We have found that if we focus on people being set free, the gifts and leadership come with a motivation that God is pleased to bless. At times I have ministered to leadership teams of larger churches and have been amazed at what is going on in the background. I thoroughly believe that healing the broken-hearted and setting the captives free was the main ministry of Jesus for a very good reason. If we want to be the church that God is pleased to anoint, we may need to consider spending a little more time on working below the water line and sorting out the areas that are not always visible.

INTRODUCTION

Learning about healing and freedom through encountering God's truth

In the early 1990s we had an elderly man in our Church who used to tell me how he had been wonderfully set free of the problems he carried. The vehicle of his freedom was a process he termed the 'healing of the memories.' He was in his 80s at the time and reported that these miraculous changes had occurred in the early 1960s. He would periodically reminisce about the amazing changes that God had brought into his life through that ministry. He was a delightful old man of God who went on to live until he was 94 years old.

In those days I did not fully understand the concept, and to be honest, at the time for me it was all about setting people free from demonic influences and teaching them to come into line with Biblical principles in order to stay free. That is still good advice, but we have come to understand that there is usually much more to the picture of being completely free than this.

Around that time, I read a book by an Australian man by the name of Thomas Foster. His publication was titled 'Miracles of Inner Healing.' This was first available in 1975 and had a subheading on the front cover stating, 'How Jesus Heals Your Memory.' Although I found the topic interesting, I was fairly convinced that what we were doing was all that was needed.

A few years later I met one of his daughters and her husband. They remain good friends to this day. They have been in ministry themselves for many years and report that they first heard Thomas Foster speak on the subject in the early 1970s. There was a later edition of the publication which I believe is still reprinted from time to time today. Later I went on to find two books on the priority of inner healing, written by David Seamands entitled; 'Healing for Damaged Emotions.' (First printing 1981), and the second entitled 'Healing of Memories' (First printing 1985).

Our first experiences of God healing in this way

In 1998, we had a lady booked in for a ministry session with a fear problem. At that time, 'healing of the memories' as it was called, did not fit into my World. It was still not a part of what we understood as to how to help people get the freedom that God has promised for us. We had however come to realize from the scriptures that *beginnings* were important. When the man in Mark chapter nine brought his mute son to Jesus for freedom, Jesus asked him this question,

"How long has this been happening to him?" And he said, "From childhood" (NKJV, Mark 9:21).

Another example noting beginning points would be the woman who was bent over with the Spirit of Infirmity in Luke chapter 13.

"And behold, there was a woman who had a spirit of infirmity eighteen years, and was bent over and could in no way raise herself up" (NKJV, Luke 13:11).

Something happened eighteen years ago that was an entry point for the spirit, and apparently nineteen years ago she did not have the problem.

It became clear to us that Jesus was looking for the beginning of the problem; the source of the issue. This indicated that there was some event or experience which was the starting place for what was going on now. In other words, the *beginning point* for ministry is an individual being asked to re-member and *describe* what had happened at a particular time in their lives? We knew enough from the scriptures to know that whatever problem a person came to us with, *something had happened somewhere* to produce the issue. This 'cause and effect' could be an event of some kind or possibly a generational influence behind the presenting situation.

In the case of this lady with the fear issue, we began asking questions regarding what she feared and where it had come from. It didn't take long and we accessed a memory that held the fear feeling and the belief producing the anxiety. As was my custom I prayed for her, asking God to set her free and addressing the spiritual dynamics that I believed to be behind the fear. She was sitting with her eyes closed remembering the event and focusing on the feeling of fear. Instead of simply feeling freer, we could see that she was having some changing facial expressions. After a few moments she opened her eyes and reported being peaceful in the memory and the fear being gone.

My wife and I had been watching her and looking at each other and wondering what was going on. We proceeded to ask her what had happened. She explained to us that once we had identified what she was afraid of, and prayed for her, God had given her a picture. What the picture meant to her had resolved the belief that she held about the situation in her memory. She remains a friend today. At the time of writing, it was around 20 years ago that she was set free. She has remained free of the belief that produced the fear. As an aside, pictures are 'one way' that God communicates with people. Indeed, some people 'think in pictures.'

As I thought through what happened in this time of ministry, I came to understand that she could not deal with her feelings with her conscious mind. The beliefs producing the emotions were learnt in a past event. It was a conscious event at the time that it happened, but what she decided at the time of the event went from being head knowledge and thoughts in her mind, to being beliefs that she held in her heart. I will explain this conclusion in detail in another chapter.

In any case, this ministry experience had me searching out my few books on 'Healing of the Memories' to take another look. It was also the beginning of seeing a great many people predictably and regularly being set free through this type of ministry. Since then, in Australia and across the World, we have taught and ministered this model of ministry, as being a part of what God offers, along with other streams that bring healing and freedom.

Others in ministry who were having similar experiences
Around 5 years later we began to hear of others who were having the same kind of freeing moments when trying to help people afflicted with emotional and mental issues. I began collecting their writings and video materials to glean whatever I could in order to be as effective as possible helping others.

I found that there were people doing this ministry from all kinds of Christian backgrounds. There were some using a lot of psychology terminology who did not believe in the gifts of the Spirit or that healing is for today, ranging through to people who pursue extra biblical manifestations as a component of their faith. The common denominator is that they were all good genuine people, regardless of their theological backgrounds and beliefs, who desired to serve

God in helping the broken hearted and setting the captives free. All of them were reporting some positive results, with God working through them to change people's lives.

Most of the models that I looked at had done some great work in putting together teaching and training manuals to help the body of Christ to be fully equipped in this area of ministry. I encouraged people in our church at the time to look at a variety of manuals and teachings for a balanced approach.

Some ministries experienced something in a simple prayer event as we did and then developed what had happened into extensive training courses. These studies can greatly help those who learn from books. We have, however, trained people, and seen others who would never complete a training manual, who have proven to be brilliant at setting people free once they receive some mentoring and understand some simple principles.

We progressively developed our own teaching materials, drawing directly from what I found the scriptures to say on the subject. So, although our ministry practices may be very similar to what others are doing, our basis and doctrine on the subject might be considerably different. This book is our offering and contribution to add to what others are bringing to light on this important and much needed ministry.

'Truth Encounters'

Truth Encounters, and other Biblically endorsed areas of ministry, need to be underpinned by a Statement of Faith (see appendices). We respectfully make some distinctions in our statement of faith that may perhaps be different in terms of the beliefs of other ministries doing this work. This is not pertaining to who is right, it is how we understand and experience the truths revealed in the Bible. We first heard the expression 'Truth Encounter' quite a number of years ago used by Pastor Mike Connell from New Zealand. During his address, he made a comment that sometimes we have 'Power Encounters' and at other times we have 'Truth Encounters.' It was such a good way of describing what we were experiencing in this area of ministry that we adopted the term, 'Truth Encounters.'

PART 1

HEALING THROUGH TRUTH FROM A BIBLICAL PERSPECTIVE

- You Will Indeed Be Set Free -

CHAPTER 1
Truth Encounters and 'The Fall of man'

Why does the truth make us free? We begin by considering how man came into bondage. Every activity, good or bad, that occurs in the Earth is a result of what people believe. It is the result or consequence of their choices and what they decide that they want to do. This begins at the individual level and outworks itself on the World stage with the instigation of events such as war. For everything to work in harmony, beginning with the internal workings of our bodies and extending to our relationships with God, others and even ourselves, we require TRUTH AT EVERY LEVEL OF OUR BEINGS.

Satan continues to work very hard to prevent this from happening, opposing God's perfect ways for mankind. The Bible gives us a very instructive picture of the working of Satan to bring about the fall of man, stating that,

"Now the serpent was the shrewdest of all the creatures the LORD God had made." "Really?" he asked the woman. "Did God really say you must not eat any of the fruit in the garden?" (NLT, Gen. 3:1).

What just happened? The devil just brought Adam and Eve under his counsel by deception. The deception came about by creating a perception about God's love, goodness and provision for them. 'Really,' implied that God was not caring and was in fact keeping something good from them. Clearly this was *not the truth*.

"Love does not delight in evil but rejoices with the truth" (NIV, 1 Corinthians 13:6).

We can say that what we believe and perceive to be 'true' is the basis of all wrongful behaviour and activity within the Earth today. The preceding verse implies that without truth, or if we deny the truth, we may be led into evil. Activities may seem right to us and good at the time and we often justify our acceptance of wrong doing. For Adam and Eve, this false perception created by Satan produced doubt and, as a result, they did not interpret the situation correctly. This misinterpretation led to a conclusion, from which they made a decision which produced an action. The action was disobedience; and rebellion against the Word of God. Throwing off Biblical laws and limits is known as sin.

We could summarize this simply by saying that sin comes through misinterpreting the *truth* of a situation and, consequently, what is actually best for us. For Adam and Eve, they saw that the tree *was* good. But in truth it was not good for them. They were much happier before, enjoying all of the many things God had given them in innocence and without guilt.

The devil continues to work in exactly the same way with humans to this day. He deceives us about who God really is and His attitude toward us, and then programs us with wrong beliefs about our own identities. Through this he manipulates humanity to serve and submit to him. His deception is behind every problem and area of suffering that is known to man.

Truth then, becomes the basis of freedom from captivity; it is the basis of faith which releases all of God's provision. It is the tool that sets us free and places us back over the influence of the deceiver that man has submitted to and come *under*.

Saul, later known as Paul, received direct instruction from the Lord that his ministry was going to be opening the eyes of those to whom he was to minister. They were under the power of Satan through deception, and they needed to correctly see and interpret their situation as the *beginning point* in turning back to God. The book of Acts records that the ministry would be

"... to open their eyes, in order to turn them from darkness to light, and from the power of Satan to God, that they may receive forgiveness of sins and an inheritance among those who are sanctified by faith in Me." (NKJV, Acts 26:18).

When we are converted, I believe we receive truth in our human spirit and something changes in us and in our relationship to God. We *know* we are children of God. And yet sometimes we don't feel like it. Our minds are not yet renewed and we struggle with our programming. Jesus said in John's gospel that the truth would make us free.

Specifically, *"And you shall know the truth, and the truth shall make you free."* (NKJV, John 8:32).

In practice I have found that we need truth in every area of our being, not just our minds. I will explain this in detail as we continue. In addition, Jesus promised that we are going to be freed with truth through the ministry of the Holy Spirit. He was going to want to inhabit every part of our person with truth, *all truth*. We could say then that one aspect of being 'filled with the Spirit' is to be filled with truth. Specifically,

"When the Spirit of truth comes, he will guide you into all truth" (NLT, John 16:13).

- You Will Indeed Be Set Free -

CHAPTER 2
Why Grace?

When we are led *"into all truth"* (NLT, John 16:13), we come to new understandings of the grace of God. From Adam and Eve on, we are all born under the deceptive power of Satan. I think that we can accurately state that nobody asked for this to be the case. We need to remember that God is a *just* God. As a consequence, we see Jesus going to the cross and asking the Father to

"... forgive them, for they do not know what they are doing" (Luke 23:34).

That is, forgive *us* for the things that we do that have put Him in the place of needing to pay the price for our sin. He was seemingly speaking of the people who were physically putting Him on the cross at the time, but it rings true of all sinners who made His crucifixion necessary for their redemption.

So, if I can paraphrase His request in light of the lack of truth that we have just discussed and note this as being the root of our behaviour and sin. He appears to be saying; 'Father, forgive them, for they have no knowledge of what is behind what they are doing.' In other words, they/we do not understand the beliefs that have led them to interpret the situation in the way they have, or what has caused them to take the actions that they have. He knows full well why we do what we do! So, we see Him asking for grace for us in our sin.

"For the law was given through Moses, but grace and truth came through Jesus Christ" (NKJV, John 1:17)

I propose then, that the implications of the grace of Jesus going to the cross for us is a rationale something like;

'I will fulfil your will Father and take care of their behaviour and resultant sin, but I will also send the Spirit of truth to guide them into understanding as to why they do what they are doing.'

He was making us perfect and presentable to the Father while sanctifying us through a continuing journey of receiving truth in the inner parts. We see this confirmed in Hebrews (10:14), which states that we were perfected, past tense, through the sacrifice of Jesus. *"For by one offering He has perfected forever those who are being sanctified"* (NKJV). Amen.

We are however on an ongoing journey of being made Holy through sanctification, which is postured as continuing in a present tense.

Many people confuse redemption with sanctification. Redemption is the finished work of Jesus in making us perfect before the Father. Many people somehow think that everything was finished at the cross, including healing and sanctification. The evidence is that churches are full of sick people with all sorts of emotional and behavioural problems. To support their doctrine, we would have to assume that these believers are not actually in the Kingdom and are therefore unsaved. It would also mean that the gifts that the Holy Spirit works through believers are also not necessary to facilitate promises such as healing that Jesus won for us. The truth is that, as we have been alluding to, redemption came through Jesus Christ and, through the cross, all of God's blessings are paid for and now available to us. His mission was finished but the era and work of the Holy Spirit was just about to begin. Sanctification then is the ongoing work of the Holy Spirit to us and in us.

Some people seem to believe that if we just think of ourselves as being a 'new creation' then we will be completely whole. And yet, there are many Christians who struggle with sin, sickness, wrong reactions, damaged emotions, addictions, imperfect relationships, areas of deception, fear and anxiety etc.

We are indeed a new creation, in the sense that we are spiritually connected with, and in a new place with God. We now have a heart that is sensitive to God and is desiring relationship with Him. The old life that had no interest in God has passed away. Through the sacrifice of Jesus on the cross we are now back in direct relationship with God, our potential is now unlimited.

Healing, freedom, and sanctification are now available, along with the gifts of the Spirit, to facilitate the work of God. An example of this would be; God so loved the world and Jesus died for the sins of all. Are all people in the World saved? No, although He loves the World and desires that none perish, not all love God, so not all are saved because not all access the provisions of the cross through faith. In the same way, not all believe that healing, deliverance, or the healing of a broken heart are for today or for them personally. Consequently, they do not receive the fullness of their redemption.

Mankind fell from grace as the result of doubting the integrity of God's word to us; by implication, His good intentions, love, and plans for us all. God has now limited Himself to faith to access all of His provisions. The evidence reveals that we will only receive what we believe that God has provided for us. In the event that we believe that the Word of God says what it means and means what it says, we can perhaps summarize our New Testament relationship and interaction with Him in the following way;

Redemption	=	that which God does **for** you
Sanctification	=	that which God does **in** you
Mission	=	that which God does **through** you.

After we understand what God has done for us, we can then work with Him in allowing and pursuing that which He wants to do in us! The final outworking of this will see us positioned to serve God in whatever works He has predetermined to do through us.

Grace that produces a heart response
Strong's concordance states that an aspect of the Greek word *Charis*, which is translated *grace*, is an effect of His grace as 'the divine influence on the heart.' What a beautiful picture of the work of the Spirit of truth in encouraging us to seek out God's truth for our growth as a response to all that He has done for us. Grace is given, not taken; it is not something that we should receive without thanksgiving. It should elicit in us a heart of praise and a life laid down and dedicated to God. Sadly, many miss this and, having been forgiven, return to a self-centred life as 'Lord' of their own lives.

A wonderful illustration of redemption and grace
I recently read a story about one of New York city's most popular mayors by the name of Fiorello LaGuardia. His 3-term service was during the 1930s and 40s. He reportedly was not happy about

people who exploited the poor. One bitterly cold night the mayor decided to preside over night court. An old woman was brought in charged with stealing a loaf of bread. She explained that her family was starving. LaGuardia's response was, "I've got to punish you. The law makes no exception. I must fine you ten dollars." (I worked out that in today's money, in Australia, that would be close to $300). Having said that he reached into his own pocket and paid the fine for her trespass, placing the $10 into his own hat. He then declared, "I'm going to fine everybody in this courtroom fifty cents for living in a town where a person has to steal bread in order to eat!" *As the story goes, the incredulous old woman left the courtroom with a new light in her eyes and $47.50 in her pocket to buy groceries. This could be as much as $1,500 today; a lot of groceries indeed.

It is a great picture of the Gospel. The law demanded that she be punished, but grace insisted on blessing. Indeed, the price for her trespass must be paid. But the person presiding over the law paid the price himself. The law held her accountable, but justice and righteousness held her environment and circumstances accountable.

As it is written, "**Righteousness and justice** are the foundation of Your throne; **Mercy and truth** go before Your face" (NKJV, Psalm 89:14).

What did she do to earn the great blessing and forgiveness that she left with? Nothing at all, she surely sinned. We come to God with our sin, and we walk away with so many blessings; it's amazing. Fiorello LaGuardia was looking past the sin as to why she sinned.

All have sinned but God was looking at *why* we sin. As we have just seen in Psalm 89, the very foundation of God's throne is justice. He would be denying His very nature to not extend grace and help in freeing and sanctifying a fallen and suffering humanity. Jesus paid the penalty demanded by the law, and then sent the Holy Spirit to ensure the provisions of God are received and to resolve the reasons for the offense to begin with. The mission of the Church therefore, is to serve the Father as Jesus did. We do this by ministering God's grace, co labouring with the Holy Spirit in bringing truth, freedom and healing to the captives.

Note: The basic deceptions that Satan proposed in relation to the tree of the knowledge of good and evil stand fast today as the basis for mankind agreeing to cooperate in sin. Let me summarise them as follows:
'This is what you need, this will make you happy.'
'You're missing out, good things are being kept from you.'

The tree of the knowledge of good and evil in that sense is alive and well today being strongly presented through channels such as media. In the Garden of Eden this had the added element of doubt that God really had their best interests at heart, and therefore was not really a good, loving God. Sin means to 'offend' or an offence. It is not surprising therefore that the first offence against God was doubting His person, and consequently the only way to now please Him and access His provisions is the reverse of doubt, faith.

*Gods Little Devotional Bible   HB HONOR Books

- You Will Indeed Be Set Free -

CHAPTER 3
Understanding the Biblical meaning of the 'Heart'

Before we can fully appreciate the ramifications of receiving truth in the processes of sanctification, healing and freedom, we first need to study where truth needs to be applied.

The ministry of Jesus

John 16 says that *"however, when He, the Spirit of truth, has come, He will guide you into all truth"* (NKJV, John 16:13).

The application of this passage relates to the Holy Spirit guiding us into 'ALL' truth. *All* means every area that requires truth. We tend to read this as meaning doctrinal truth, revelation, and understandings for our minds. This is certainly *a part* of how we will know the truth that will set us free. For example, hearing the good news of Christ Jesus can bring us redemption. Renewing the minds of believers is a high priority for the modern church in an information-based world. There is no doubting that this is very important for learning and following the ways of God. The disengaging of the World is, no doubt, the responsibility of the believer in disciplining their mind to the things of God. We certainly need to be *hearers* and *doers* in terms of knowing how we should live and act. We have a mandate as follows:

"And do not be conformed to this world but be transformed by the renewing of your mind" (NKJV, Romans 12:2).

The heart

There is another area of our being that is however largely neglected by the modern church. This part of our person also requires truth, and is often directly related to us receiving wholeness and freedom. Once He had received the Holy Spirit, Jesus announced amongst other things that He was going to 'Heal the broken hearted,' and 'set the captives free.' He was quoting Isaiah 61 where the Old Testament prophet had listed what the activities of Jesus would be when the Holy Spirit came upon Him. Notably these words had not previously been fulfilled; it required that there was a person aligned with the Word and will of the Father whom the Holy Spirit could work through. With the coming of Jesus as Christ the result was that the Isaiah 61 Word became flesh and had a manifestation and expression in the Earth.

We read in Luke 4, "[18] *The Spirit of the LORD is upon Me, Because He has anointed Me To preach the gospel to the poor; He has sent Me* **to heal the broken-hearted**, *To proclaim liberty to the captives And recovery of sight to the blind, To set at liberty those who are oppressed;* [19] *To proclaim the acceptable year of the LORD*" (NKJV, Luke 4:18-19, emphasis mine).

Jesus modelled to us how to walk in the Spirit in terms of behaviour and attitudes, as well as how to minister in the Spirit, expressing the gifts of the Spirit. He did no works of His own ability and began His own ministry when He received the Holy Spirit and began to be led by the Spirit.

What He introduced to us was meant to be the beginning of the Luke 4:18-19 ministries for mankind and not the end. The plan was that Spirit led believers would continue the works and example modelled by Jesus. This is very much the reason the Spirit of the LORD is upon us today. We read,

"*So Jesus said to them again, 'Peace to you! As the Father has sent Me, I also send you. And when He had said this, He breathed on them, and said to them, 'Receive the Holy Spirit'*" (NKJV, John 20:21-22).

The Gospels do not directly tell us how He healed the Broken Hearted. We do understand that the words that He spoke to people were powerful to heal, in that He was and is God Himself. Today, we still see people receive their healing when they receive a word from the Spirit of Christ. Some people struggle with this concept, but it is as simple as; 'my sheep hear my voice.' In fact, believers will seek to listen diligently knowing that His words are Spirit and life. John states,

"*It is the Spirit who gives life; the flesh profits nothing. The words that I speak to you are spirit, and they are life*" (NKJV, John 6:63).

Further, Jesus promised that when we know *the* truth it will make us free. Specifically,

"And you shall know the truth, and the truth shall make you free" (NKJV, John 8:32).
What is the Biblical function of the 'Heart'?

"And you shall love the LORD your God with all your **heart***, with all your* **soul***, with all your* **mind***, and with all your* **strength***. This is the first commandment"* (NKJV, Mark 12:30, emphasis mine).

Here are four clear and distinct areas that the Bible reveals as individual in function. Your *strength* is considered to be your forcefulness, ability, might or power. Your *soul* is generally accepted to be your mind, will and emotions in terms of the sum of whom you are as a person; I think, I will and I feel.

In this passage your *mind* is also singled out and the word that it is translated from, means, your capacity and faculty to be able to reason, understand, and imagine. It has the ability of conscious thought leading to conclusions. For example, it has the function of being able to compute and think through a mathematical problem and to produce an answer. It is very much a conscious activity and would include deliberately memorizing and voluntarily storing information. We could summarize the *mind* as your thinker or your computer which has the ability to store or access information.

We come now to what the Bible refers to as our *heart*. For the sake of the study, I will quote the function and operation of the *heart*, as translated from the Greek directly from the very reputable Strong's Concordance.

2588. kardia; the heart, i.e. (fig.) the thoughts or feelings (mind); also (by anal.) the middle: --(+ broken-) heart (-ed) (Emphasis mine).

It appears from the original language that the scripture is referring to a deeper area of the personality that holds thoughts which produce feelings and behaviour. I am proposing that these thoughts and feelings are coming from beliefs that were once conscious thoughts or beliefs involuntarily learnt by experiences and events. They were significant conclusions or interpretations arrived at in the past that are stored or *taken* to heart. These thoughts, beliefs or feelings have usually come as a result of the programming of life, as deliberate training or experiential beliefs stemming from events.

We may no longer know them as beliefs or thoughts but rather as feelings, behaviour or responses to particular situations. This is further confirmed in the Bible with the statement that the word of God is able to access this deeper place. Hebrews 4, verse 12 states,

*"For the word of God is living and active. Sharper than any double-edged sword, it penetrates even to dividing soul and spirit, joints and marrow; it judges the thoughts and attitudes **of the heart**".* (NIV, Hebrews 4:12, emphasis mine).

So evidently our *hearts* have thoughts and attitudes that need to be discerned or judged. Jesus actually named one means of doing this as listening to what people are saying. We can measure this against the word of God to see if the thought, intent, motivation or attitude is correct. For example, someone may be heard saying; "that's just how it is with me, I'm never going to be good enough." And yet, the word of God says that we are His creation and through Jesus we are just fine as we are! However, we discern that the preceding thought and statement is sourced from the heart. Scripture says,

*"You brood of vipers, how can you who are evil say anything good? For out of the **overflow of the heart** the mouth speaks"* (NIV, Matthew 12:34, emphasis mine).

It is a principle that often the words that come out of us locate us in terms of what our inner beliefs are. The New Living Translation presents it in this way:

"For whatever is in your heart determines what you say" (NLT, Matthew 12:34b).

Our heart, or *middle* as Strong's concordance describes, has a lot to do with how we live, act and react. Consequently, it is vital to have truth in our hearts in order to experience wholeness and abundance in our lives. 1 Corinthians 4:5 says:

*"Therefore, judge nothing before the appointed time; wait till the Lord comes. He will bring to light what is hidden in darkness and will expose the **motives** of men's **hearts**. At that time each will receive his praise from God"* (NIV, 1 Corinthians 4:5, emphasis mine).

Let me suggest some of the outworking's and implications proceeding from the beliefs held in the heart. In fact, we have found that every kind of problem known to man can be found *beginning* here. As a sweeping statement, this includes things that we suffer as a result of the condition of other people's hearts. This is clearly confirmed in scripture:

"Above all else, guard your heart, for it affects everything you do" (NLT, Proverbs 4:23).

Above all else, protecting what goes into your heart is a compelling and vitally important instruction; this includes whatever we allow in through our conscious decisions. We can consistently and deliberately expose ourselves to the things of God through voluntary activities such as storing up the word of God, or we can be conformed to the World by various forms of media and exposure to negative influences. May I suggest that perhaps the 'heart' is the middle, central point or junction of the soul. That is the mind, will and emotions, and consequently it has a direct affect and influence on the function of them all.

- You Will Indeed Be Set Free -

CHAPTER 4
The role of memory

Voluntary and involuntary memory

Voluntary memory
Permit me to introduce some terms that we can use to help us understand the different ways that we can have things *stored up* in our hearts. One way is that we have information that we have decided to consciously learn and then retain through repetition. This could include the 10 times table or the scriptures. We could also have memory that affects us from Worldly things that we have decided to expose ourselves to. These things which we have taken into our hearts will have an influence on how we live by way of future decisions, motivations, activities and behaviour. This kind of memory or *heart belief* is to do with how we shape what we understand and perceive about the world around us. It pertains to things such as our morality, skills, and functionality.

Automatized thinking
As an adult, most likely if you exit your shower or bath and begin to dry yourself with a towel, it will not be a deliberate conscious exercise. You are possibly thinking about how your day will go or something else. At one time when you were learning how to dry yourself, it was a deliberate conscious effort involving your mind. Now if you involve your conscious thought with something like, "do I dry this arm or this arm next?", you might find that your minds involvement creates confusion with your processes that are now automatic.

I quite like music, and as an adult I will sometimes memorize a song in order to be able to just play it. I find that if I just let it come out of my heart it happens automatically, but if I begin to consciously think about which note is coming up next, I almost always mess it up.

Many of the feelings, responses, decisions and activities that we go through are done automatically in this way. For example, the mental activity of deciding what is suitable for us to watch on TV. It was once something that we worked out with our conscious mind, but now our responses and actions come automatically from the conclusions and interpretations about life that *we already hold in our hearts*. Jesus very emphatically stated that many of our actions come from the prior encoding of this deeper place.

Matthew says, *"But the things that come out of the mouth* **come from the heart**, *and these make a man 'unclean.'* **For out of the heart** *come evil thoughts, murder, adultery, sexual immorality, theft, false testimony, slander"* (NIV, Matthew 15:18-19, emphasis mine).

We could quite easily add a large number of good and bad deeds that come from the heart to that list. Jesus was just giving us a sample of negative activities that come from what has been stored in the heart. It is worth considering as the modern church that Jesus really took the Pharisees to task for focusing on outward appearances and neglecting dealing with *the issues of the heart* in the people they were responsible for. They were giving them religious rules on how they should look and what they should do, instead of helping them find freedom by a relationship with God and accessing His provisions through the Holy Spirit. That is not to say that we don't want to present well as a church, but we need to major on ministering to the broken hearted as Jesus did.

"Then the Lord said to him, "Now you Pharisees make the outside of the cup and dish clean, but your **inward part is full of greed and wickedness"""** (NKJV, Luke 11:39, emphasis mine).

A little later he admonished them for giving them outward religion and rules without setting them free from the problems that have caused their negative behaviour to begin with. Religion is seen as follows; 'This is what you do to be right with, or please God!' or 'This is how you do it, how you should look, what you should say!' These are human created standards and efforts for practicing Christianity.

"Yes," said Jesus, "how terrible it will be for you experts in religious law! For you crush people beneath impossible religious demands, and you never lift a finger to help ease the burden" (NLT, Luke 11:46).

Involuntary memory
Involuntary memory is beliefs that you have taken into your heart that were not intentionally or purposefully learnt. These beliefs

have also become 'automatized' and so we no longer know them as conscious thoughts or beliefs; we may now know them as only feelings, emotions or responses and behaviour.

Remember our definition of 'the heart' as being *thoughts and feelings* from our *middle or central part*. These may come to us involuntarily through experiential learning in, for example, feelings of rejection received in a historical event, or perhaps fear, anger or inferiority learnt through life.

We have already stated that the conscious mind interprets events and comes to conclusions which then become beliefs that are stored in our *hearts*. These beliefs that are in our hearts are recorded there usually through repetition or significant events. In terms of critical matters such as our identity and how we think others view us, the Bible tells us that we are most influenced as children. Science confirms what the Bible has always said, that a child's brain is plastic and formative in terms of self-awareness and identity up until around 10 years old. In Hebrew, **a child** is regarded to be between infancy and adolescence. Adolescence is considered to begin at around 10 years old, so biblically a child is less than 10 years old.

"Train a child in the way he should go, and when he is old he will not turn from it" (NIV, Proverbs 22:6).

20 years and thousands of hours of ministry have confirmed that most people's identity beliefs, proceed from situations, that have been found in the heart and are sourced in memories before the age of 10 years old. An *identity belief* is one that has to do with who you 'are' and how you perceive that others see you. It is *your* reality or *truth* about your- 'self.' Very often a spirit other than the Holy Spirit has helped you interpret life and come to the conclusion that you now hold about yourself. Even in a Christian household those who were meant to help *guard our hearts* may have unintentionally been the source of our programming.

Many people have grown up in households where as a child you were informed that; 'little children should be seen and not heard!' At that moment you have had fed into your heart that you are some kind of lesser humanity that should not have a voice.

Situational beliefs
A *situational belief* is one that has come from an event or theme in life that has programmed you to believe something which could affect how you perceive your identity, but also how you feel about life in general. Many children today are in a situation where a parent has left them and gone out of the home. Their experience has perhaps taught them that, 'people cannot be trusted to care about you, you are not safe or important.'

A *sample of identity beliefs includes*: 'I am not loved/lovable, I am worthless, not good enough, not important, I am a nothing, I don't matter,' etc. etc.

A *sample of situational beliefs includes*: 'There is no one there to protect me; no one cares about me, nobody wants me, I am not as good as others, I won't be able to do it,' etc.

Repetition
Reportedly the brain has little cells called 'Microglial' cells which account for 10-15% of all of the cells found in the brain. A part of their function is to clear up cellular debris. They are like little vacuum cleaners that go through your brain and suck up and dispose of useless information that is not reinforced within 24 to 48 hours. General information is considered important enough to be kept *through repetition*. We see this with the ten times table, or perhaps repeatedly being dealt with in a particular way while growing up. This will program and reinforce what you believe to the point of it becoming a permanent belief.

A Biblical example can be found with God telling Joshua five times to be strong and courageous. He seems to be saying; 'you need to meditate on this, take it to heart, and make it your default position, because when you see those angry guys with spears coming over the hill you will need to have your default position and response settled way down deep inside of you. Then you don't need to think about it because you have it as an *automatic* response.

Critical moments or events
Information deeply encoded in *significant* emotional or traumatic *events*, including moments of weakness, or episodes containing fear

or extreme stress, are taken to heart and remain. Most seventy-year old's will not remember what they had for breakfast on their first day of school. There is no reason for your brain to store in memory that information as it has no real bearing on your life. They may however remember beliefs recorded through interpreting events related to the anxieties of the day, and the acceptance of others in a new environment.

We have found that anything that you can remember from your childhood was a significant moment in either a positive way or negative way. It may have been a time where you were coming to some conclusion about yourself or your situation. Once you have decided that you are, for example, inferior you are going to interpret future situations in the same way. It is a *heart belief* that you now carry and you are, in a sense, what you think you are in your heart. You will make your decisions based on those beliefs. For example, if you have learnt through experience that you are not very smart with remembering words you will probably avoid spelling contests like the plague. They will only potentially confirm what you already believe about yourself and expose that perceived weakness to everyone else.

Significant emotional or traumatic events are burned deeply into your memory through an electro-chemical process called protein synthesis. This could be events such as being embarrassed in a school room, a fearful event of perhaps nearly drowning, and range through to the trauma of seeing porn on a smart phone where the deeply recorded images can reportedly last a lifetime.

- You Will Indeed Be Set Free -

CHAPTER 5
Grasshoppers and faith

"For as he thinks in his heart, so is he. "Eat and drink!" he says to you, But his heart is not with you" (NKJV, Proverbs 23:7).

Notice that this passage does not state *as the man thinks in his mind*. The passage suggests that the man has invited you for a meal and that is the good intention that he has towards you. But he has a conflict between his conscious choice and what is going on for him at heart level. Perhaps he heard a great message about hospitality at church and is trying to live it out, however he grew up in a poor household where they often didn't have enough to eat. That which he now wills to do is in conflict with the anxiety coming from his previous experiences and the beliefs held inside him about there being enough. The reality may well be that he has plenty but he is going to default to his previous programming every time.

As he thinks in his heart, so is he. A profound old saying puts it this way: **'It's not what you think you are, but WHAT YOU THINK, you ARE!'** In other words, you will live your life according to what you think about yourself. Let us reinforce this thought by repeating the scripture from Proverbs,
"Above all else, guard your heart, for it affects everything you do" (NLT, Proverbs 4:23).

A great example of this in the scriptures is that of the Israelites. While God was doing everything, they were doing fine. It is the picture of redemption where God performs the complete activity for them in delivering them from the slavery and the subservience that they were under in Egypt. In the same way God does everything through Jesus and delivers us from the slavery of the law and sin.

God was then looking for them to participate with Him in occupying a land that He had set apart for them. He even tells them that He had gone before them and had given them the land. By faith they can walk into their inheritance. It would be wonderful, and they all agree that it is a good land. So, what is the problem, what holds them back from entering into this promised life walking in the provision

of God? Numbers 13:33 records the problem as a reconnaissance report stating,
"We even saw giants there, the descendants of Anak. We felt like grasshoppers next to them, and that's what we looked like to them!" (NLT).

The Israelites had grown up as slaves. They had grown up with low self-image and inferiority as they were being treated as some kind of lesser beings. This lack of confidence now emanated out of them and was discerned by their potential opponents.

Often people criticize the modern church for its lack of faith and power. Remember that many have grown up in a broken, rejective family and society. Like the Israelites, they would like to move into the Promised Land but they have been taught that they are not good enough, or not worthy to carry God's power and provision. They need first to be set free at a heart level.

The Promised Land for believers is the 'abundant life to the full' that Jesus announced He came to bring. Sadly, just as with the Israelites, many never come into it because of their **unbelief**, that is, **wrong belief** about themselves and how God sees them. They give mental assent to the scriptures but can never exercise heart faith and trust in God to live the life that He wants for them. It is noteworthy that Jesus said that we can have whatever we believe in our hearts as opposed to what we believe with our minds.

Mark 11:23 says, *"For assuredly, I say to you, whoever says to this mountain, 'Be removed and be cast into the sea,' and **does not doubt in his heart**, but believes that those things he says will be done, he will have whatever he says"* (NKJV, emphasis mine).

Doubt comes from a wrong belief about God. It began with Adam and Eve who doubted God's integrity and genuinely perfect intentions for them. It started with 'did God really say?' When we hold wrong beliefs about God at a heart level, we may hear a great inspirational message about what we should be doing, and then decide as a mental activity to try, having been convinced in our minds, only to be disappointed because we do not really believe God for the outcome.

Genuine faith is not about what you can get God to do for you by believing Him for something. True faith is about having a correct picture of who He is and His plan for you. Often, we need to hear His voice, as Jesus did, before He began His ministry confirming that you are His child and that He is pleased with you. He may not be pleased with everything you do but He is most likely pleased with who you are. He understands why you do what you do even though you do not. If your heart condemns you, God is greater than your heart.

People often quote that faith comes through hearing, and hearing the Word of God, and encourage you to read your bible more to grow in faith. In the Greek language there is the word 'logos' which is the written word of God, and the word 'Rhema' which refers to the spoken word of God. The Romans passage that we are discussing uses the word 'Rhema.'

Romans 10:17 says, *"So then faith comes by hearing, and hearing by the word (Rhema) of God"* (NKJV, emphasis mine).

So, faith or trust in God comes to us when God speaks to us in some way. This could include reading the Word at times if the Holy Spirit is highlighting a passage. But in regards to bringing truth to your heart, it is when God speaks to what you believe that your picture of God and yourself consistently changes. This releases true trust and faith in Him.

- You Will Indeed Be Set Free -

CHAPTER 6
'Strongholds' and spiritual warfare

Many years ago, we were ministering through Micronesia and our host took us for a tour around the Island of Guam. He showed us the concrete bunkers that the Japanese had built before the coming battle in order to hold the ground or territory that they occupied. The Bible says in Ephesians chapter 4 and verse 7 to not give the devil a place. The Greek word translated as 'place' is the word, topos. It means a place, a location, a position, a spot or a home.

In much the same way as the Japanese made strongholds **before** the battle began, the devil establishes ***a place*** in our belief systems through deception and misinterpretation. Later, as the Apostle Paul found out, when the Spirit of truth comes on the scene there is an internal battle and conflict for the ground or place of the heart that has already been occupied.

Many people believe that when they are feeling bad or anxious that they are under some kind of spiritual or demonic attack. Most times what is actually happening is that beliefs that the person already holds are being stressed or triggered through the environment or situation that they find themselves in. Perhaps they are confused by Paul's later statement in Ephesians regarding wrestling spiritual powers which states

"11 Put on the full armor of God so that you can take your stand against the devil's schemes. 12 For our struggle is not against flesh and blood, but against the rulers, against the authorities, against the powers of this dark world and against the spiritual forces of evil in the heavenly realms" (NIV, Ephesians 6:11-12).

In fact, he is more likely to be making reference to the fact that, although you are dealing with humans, flesh and blood, it is the negative spiritual dynamics projecting from them onto you that is your problem. In other words, it is not the people themselves that are attacking you. It is the spirits manipulating the people through their areas of deception which give place and cooperation with the powers that you are actually dealing with.

Jesus floated the concept of human participation with spiritual inspiration at various times in the gospels. It is wrong believing that opens us to being potential unwitting hosts to unholy spirit. This is exemplified in the following passage:

"*54 And when His disciples James and John saw this, they said, "Lord, do You want us to command fire to come down from heaven and consume them, just as Elijah did?" 55 But He turned and rebuked them, and said, "You do not know what manner of spirit you are of"* (NKJV, Luke 9:54-55).

In other words, James and John were not aware of what type of spirit they were cooperating with. Peter was inspired by the Spirit of God but was soon found to be working for the other side. This is true of all of us. People can do something wonderful in the love of God, and later be heard gossiping, criticizing or judging another believer. The truth is that, if we don't get our hearts cleaned out, we can at times be found to be double agents and on occasion working unintentionally for the other side! In contrast,

"He said to them, "But who do you say that I am?" Simon Peter answered and said, "You are the Christ, the Son of the living God." Jesus answered and said to him, "Blessed are you, Simon Bar-Jonah, for flesh and blood has not revealed this to you, but My Father who is in heaven" (NKJV, Matthew 16:15-17).

Peter had a wonderful Rhema word from the Father. A few short verses later, his inspiration was coming from another source which he was open to, through his previous programming in life. I am fairly sure that Jesus, much to Peter's dismay, was addressing the spirit behind the idea. This would have been quite confronting for Peter to be exposed for his co-operation and deception.

"*22 Then Peter took Him aside and began to rebuke Him, saying, "Far be it from You, Lord; this shall not happen to You!" 23 But He turned and said to Peter, "Get behind Me, Satan! You are an offense to Me, for you are not mindful of the things of God, but the things of men""* (NKJV, Matthew 16:22-23).

It is clear that very often the things that men have in mind are inspired by Satan. Nothing spiritual happens on Earth without human participation, this includes the works of God. There will be prayers and deeds motivated by faith behind Gods activities as well. When people are rejective, competing or putting you down for example, and you are feeling anxious or depressed it is most likely tapping into a belief that you already hold and not a spiritual attack.

CHAPTER 7
Beliefs produce feelings or what we term emotions

We have seen that the Israelites were unable to take up their destiny because of beliefs of inferiority which produced feelings of fear and inadequacy. If they had instead been programmed by life that they were equal or if they had received healing from their previous beliefs, they would have felt confident and full of faith! Sadly, the covenant that they were under did not include the ministry of the Spirit of truth, so they did not have the opportunity for freedom from their inner thoughts that we find ourselves with.

Thoughts and feelings
A feeling or emotion is the result of a belief that has been accessed. In fact, it is your chemical bodies' version of what you believe. So, a thought or belief and feelings or emotions are one and the same. Some time ago I was reading a book where Charles Finney made the statement that 'feelings follow thoughts.' This is a profound statement in its application to what we are discussing about the heart. You do not simply have a feeling because you have a feeling. It is emanating from something that you already believe:

- If you believe that nobody loves you, then you will feel sad.
- If you believe that no one cares about you, you may feel angry.
- If you think that there is no protection for you, your emotion will probably be anxiety.
- If you believe that you will never ever be able to be what people expect you to be, then you will feel overwhelmed and hopeless, which is the basis of endogenous depression. Endogenous meaning, having an internal origin.

Proverbs 12:25 says, *"Anxiety in the heart of man causes depression, But a good word makes it glad"* (NKJV, emphasis mine).

A feeling or emotion is a chemical elaboration of a belief through the release of hormones or neurotransmitters. It is a thought or belief that your body makes into a feeling or emotion through these chemicals. For example, a fear belief will release particular hormones such as adrenaline and the stress hormone, cortisol, so that your body can make your thoughts something that you can feel. These hormones have other functions in your bodies so when you have long term negative emotions, they become imbalanced, and this is the basis for disease.

Two little boys
In order to help people understand this principle, I often use the following story when I am preparing them for ministry. There were two little 5-year-old boys walking down a street in their town. One of them noticed a motorbike across the road and went over to look at it. As the other boy continued down the road a dog came out of the gateway of a nearby house and bit him on the leg. In that moment of trauma, it was deeply encoded in him that dogs can hurt and frighten you. His mind has made a very good memory of the event, and he is now on guard against the possibility of it happening again. In order to counteract this ever-present fear, he reads numerous books about how dogs are man's best friend and that most of them will never hurt you. He is trying to counteract his involuntary heart belief with voluntary information from his mind.

This is often what we do in church and wonder why people never change or have limited growth. We give them lots of information to learn for their problems and tell them how they should think, perhaps sometimes not unlike the Pharisees. The Jesus model was to heal their broken hearts and set the captives free. I will explain what I mean by this statement a little further on, but back to our story for the moment.

As he grows up and becomes a teenager he is often invited to his friends' houses and really wants to go, but underneath there is a nagging hesitation and anxiety. He is not consciously thinking it but underneath the thought that there may be a dog at their house is producing the anxiety. So, his inner beliefs are beginning to affect his life choices.

Many years later the 5-year-old boys are again together walking and are now 40 years old. As they go along a small dog comes out of a laneway near them wagging his tail. The man who was bitten has an immediate physical fear response, even though with his mind he is trying frantically to apply the knowledge that he has about dogs and is telling himself how it looks so friendly. His heart belief that dogs sometimes bite you is greater than his logical conscious knowledge that the dog looks really friendly. The outworking is the release of fear hormones and a very uncomfortable feeling in his physical body.

His friend on the other hand has an entirely different response. He feels happy, warm and 'fuzzy.' What is the difference; it's the same dog? Growing up as a small boy, his family had a friendly dog that played with him, climbed all over him and licked his face. The emotions that he was feeling were coming from different beliefs about the situation stored in his heart. So, the same situation was producing opposing responses based on what they already believed.

Captivity
Many people are tormented and held captive to beliefs that they hold about themselves, their worth, or their situations. For example, a number of years ago we had a black dog we called 'Misty.' As a pup she used to go out of the yard and get lost if we weren't home. As a result, if we went out, we would tie a rope to her collar and connect it to a fence post to keep her from running away. Of course, she tried to get loose for a while but eventually gave up. When she was older, I would tie the rope to her collar but not bother to tie up the other end. She no longer tried to get away; she had attempted to before and learnt that it was impossible. She was captive in her thinking to her previous situation.

This was now belief-based behaviour or responses. This was not necessarily an emotion for her anymore although originally it may have been frustration. Now it was belief-based behaviour that she was captive to.

Many people are held captive to what they perceive to be true. These inner thoughts indeed may come from an episode or training that at one time was true. A lot of actions, activities and responses come from previous programming, and although consciously with our minds we want to do something, we find that we cannot do what we want to do, there is something opposing us.

The Apostle Paul came to understand this clearly in his own walk. Many people like him wish to follow the things of God as they come into a New Creation potential, being on a new footing with a reborn spirit. They now have the Holy Spirit to guide them, and the word of God to instruct them. Just like Paul however, they often find themselves with one foot on the accelerator and one foot on the brake.

A program behind the program
In our early days of teaching this ministry I was operating one of the first versions of Microsoft PowerPoint from my Laptop computer to facilitate the presentation. My computer was not running properly and was taking a very long time to perform normally simple tasks. The man who had sold me the computer was actually in the congregation and so I invited him up to the platform to resolve the issue. He took one look at the computer and pointed to a little green light that was flashing. "There," he said, "there is a program running behind the program, and that is why it is not functioning properly!" With that he, with a blur of hands across the keyboard, far too fast to ever remember what he did, turned off the 'scanning' program that was operating in the background. It was going on underneath, with no obvious evidence on the screen other than its poor operation and the little green light flickering. This was a light bulb moment for me. I suddenly understood Romans 7 and the Apostle Paul's dilemma in a new way. Not only his discomfort but also many other Christians who want to live according to the word of God.

There is something going on in the background that is affecting the operation of the will. This other 'program' needs to be switched off by the Holy Spirit before you can be all that you can be and do all that you choose to do without hindrance.

If you can imagine the screen as the conscious mind which will only display what you actively choose to think about. If you think about fruit or perhaps a hot dog, you will now have something on the screen of your conscious mind. But while you think about what you have decided to think about, behind this may be feelings of anxiety or depression coming from a deeper place, your *heart*, that are not conscious. These are other programs behind what you are deciding to do with your mind need to be addressed. You want to think and react in all of the ways that you see in scripture with your conscious mind but something else is in play.

I sometimes think that we read in the Bible, for example, about the fruit of the Spirit as ways that we should decide to act. This is certainly true in the sense of our conscious decisions, but in practice these fruits are more often the results of the work that the Holy Spirit has done in our hearts. We could use the example of choosing to be joyful, but for many, this will be impossible without being made free from beliefs producing guilt, shame, inadequacy or anxiety.

CHAPTER 8
The example of the Apostle Paul's Dilemma

In Romans chapter 7:15-25, we see a battle going on in the 'members' or different areas of the Apostle Paul's being. This is the case for many people in the church today. Let us summarize the problem in this way. Their spirit is reborn of the Holy Spirit, (John 3:5-8) so they are now connected to the Father and the Kingdom of God, but there are areas where wrong believing still has 'a place.' They are hungry for the truth and want to live out the Word of God as a response to the leading of the Holy Spirit. So spiritually they are willing, and in their conscious minds they want to walk after God. However, pulling against them is their old programming. They have what they know and confess to be true from the word of God, but it is not setting them free. They appear to be double minded. Their confession, and their responses, behaviour and actions do not match.

These people are on a journey of renewing their minds with truth, but another part of them is defaulting to their old ways of acting. Their bodies and hearts want to continue to conform to the responses, attitudes, motivations, habits and associations that have been programmed into them through life in the World.

In order to understand this clearly, in the following verses from Romans Chapter 7 let's make **his renewed spirit man, under the influence of the Holy Spirit** to be in bold letters to make a distinction. In order to see the opposing nature of his 'flesh' person we will underline it where it presents.
(Note: We understand that his '_flesh_' or Sarx in the Greek language is what I propose is largely his unsanctified and previously programmed heart. As we have already alluded to, this is where Jesus says that the nature of sin proceeds from. See Mathew 15:18-19 and Luke 11:39. This is also sometimes translated or referred to as the sin nature, Adamic, Carnal or fallen nature. I like to think of it for the sake of simplicity as; the fallen self-life, or the old life.)

"I don't understand _myself_ at all, for I really want to do what is right, but _I don't_ do it. Instead, _I do_ the very thing I hate" (NLT, Romans 7:15, emphasis mine).

It is like that person in church who hears a message on forgiveness. A part of them wants to forgive and be in line with the Kingdom, and they even know that they should. But another part of them wants to justify itself and hold on to the resentment. Internal peace is gone as flesh clashes with spirit.

Mostly, the truth in this case is that whatever the person who is not being forgiven is doing or has done is not the main problem. The issue is usually that something that is offending is touching a belief that the person holds, and this causes some kind of emotional reaction. For example, you may not be forgiving a spouse for seeming to not care about your needs. The probability is that somewhere in your history you were treated as though you do not matter or are not important. So, the real issue behind the resentful response that you are trying not to have, is the pain of believing that you do not matter for some reason. The unforgiveness is the *fruit* of the hurt that is held and not the actual root of the behaviour.

The problem then is the belief that is held in the unsanctified or unhealed part of the heart. The Spirit of truth has to bring truth, healing and sanctification to this belief before that area of the heart can come into harmony under the covering of the Spirit. Otherwise it will continue to contest what kind of behaviour is most appropriate as a response to life situations. This appears to be the kind of dilemma that Paul was found in.

" 22 For I delight in the law of God according to the inward man. 23 But I see another law in <u>my members</u>, warring against the law of my mind, and bringing <u>me</u> into captivity to the law of sin which is in <u>my members</u>" (NKJV, Romans 7:22-23 emphasis mine).

Let us try to give another picture of what this could look like in practice. A person is waiting for the Sunday church service to begin. The Pastor or minister comes in and walks right past them without the least sign of recognition. The person feels quite upset but tries to tell themselves that it is ok, and not to worry about it. It's all good, after all they have lots of friends. It happens again the next week and they have a little anger and begin to notice little faults with the minister and shares them with others. **They** know that *they* should not be doing this, but what **they** know *they* should not do, *they* do. What is happening here?

The person knows that they should forgive the minister. If they looked at and identified that upset feeling they would find that they are being made to feel unimportant. An area that does not yet have truth, that has previously been programmed, teaching them that they are unimportant is being accessed. Out of them are coming retaliatory responses that they know are wrong but that they cannot seem to stop. The *truth* is that they have misinterpreted the situation, believing and holding a perception that the minister did not value them. In actual fact the minister considers them a valuable part of the church family, but immediately before the service he is trying to make sure that all the music is in order, the preaching is ready to go, and the equipment is all working and so on.

Is this resolved by the person trying harder to solve their concern? They are already trying as hard as they can to go with their convictions from scripture about how they should be, and they are feeling condemned because they cannot seem to resolve it with their good intentions, knowledge of scripture, and their own efforts to work it out with their minds.

"[24] *Oh, what a miserable person I am! Who will free* me *from this life that is dominated by sin?* [25] *Thank God! The answer is in Jesus Christ our Lord*" (NLT, Romans 7:24-25).

The answer is Jesus Christ our Lord. So how can we be free?
King David made a profound statement in regards to God's intentions and method for healing, sanctifying and freeing us. When he talks about God's desire for truth in the inner parts, you will see how this lines up with healing broken hearts, setting the captives free and working through the process of sanctification. *Inner parts* in the Old Testament scripture that we are about to quote can, according to Hebrew scholars, also be translated as *the heart*. The *inmost place* refers to the human spirit. Personally, I believe that our re-born human spirit already receives and witnesses to the truth of God's word by the work of the Holy Spirit. However, our hearts or inner parts need the truth that God wants us to know in order for us to be set free.

Psalm 51:5-6 says, "[5] *Surely I was sinful at birth, sinful from the time my mother conceived me.* [6] *Surely you desire truth in the inner parts; you teach me wisdom in the inmost place*" (NIV).

Noteworthy, King David acknowledges the passing of the sin nature through the generations to him right at the point of conception. The King also acknowledged that it was his heart that needed cleaning. Psalm 51 was written following David's sin with Bathsheba. Somehow, he had for some time managed to deny his sin and contrived some way to justify his behaviour. Many people seem to be content to live on the surface of their being not seeking out the root reason for their activities. As Jeremiah 17:9-10 states,

"*9 The heart is deceitful above all things, And desperately wicked; Who can know it? 10 I, the LORD, search the heart, I test the mind. Even to give every man according to his ways, According to the fruit of his doings*" (NKJV).

It becomes very apparent that each of us need to let the LORD search our hearts, as most often we are not aware of why we do what we do, or where it is coming from. We can join with King David in inviting the Holy Spirit to help us find out what we believe at a heart level and set us free. It is like putting the anti-virus program on your computer to remove the corrupted files so that the machine runs how it was intended. Scripture says,

"*Create in me a clean heart, O God, And renew a steadfast spirit within me*" (NKJV, Psalm 51:10).

Adam and Eve ran *from* God. Through Jesus we can now run boldly to God for freedom through His truth in our hearts. Psalm 139:23-24 expresses this desire as follows;

"*23 Search me, O God, and know my heart; test me and know my thoughts. 24 Point out anything in me that offends you, and lead me along the path of everlasting life*" (NLT).

CHAPTER 9
Sanctification, healing & freedom come through truth

We have already quoted the verse that *the truth will make us free*. This freedom begins by acknowledging that our captivity comes through what we believe that is not truth. Such as not understanding sound doctrine in regards to our minds but also importantly what we hold to be true at heart level. It is clear that sanctification comes through truth from God.

John says, *"Sanctify them by Your truth. Your word is truth"* (NKJV, John 17:17).

That is a fairly unchallengeable and straightforward statement. Our minds are renewed by truth and our hearts are healed and released from captivity to wrong beliefs in the same way. If then, sanctification comes through truth, it is fair to deduce that being guided into truth by the Spirit of truth is the way of sanctification at every level.

"When the Spirit of truth comes, he will guide you into all truth" (NLT, John 16:13).

This is why we have come to refer to this ministry as 'Truth Encounters.' It is when we have an encounter with the Holy Spirit and He reveals truth to us. He speaks to us as sheep who hear His voice and we are changed. The Holy Spirit has been sent to us through Jesus, who has extended us grace for our sins, but also is influencing our hearts to seek and walk in the truth. As previously stated, Strong's concordance presents Charis, the word from which grace is translated in the following manner.

485. charis,; from G5463; graciousness; lit., fig. or spiritual; espec. (the divine influence upon the heart) acceptable, benefit, favor, gift, grace

It appears from the Bible that the very reason for the coming of Jesus was to bring us the grace of God, and then restore us to wholeness through the truth. The ministry of the Holy Spirit then in this era is vital in every way.

"For the law was given through Moses, but grace and truth came through Jesus Christ" (NKJV, John 1:17).

CHAPTER 10
What is a Broken Heart and who are the broken hearted?

Let us first examine God's priority regarding those suffering in this area. We have already identified from the Greek language in the New Testament that the *heart* is beliefs or thoughts that are manifested or matched by corresponding feelings or emotions. In the Old Testament the word that is translated as *heart* from the Hebrew language *Leb* also relates to your centre, your intellect, will and is widely used for feelings.

The central place of motivation for your inner thoughts, which produce feelings and influence your decisions and responses, is your *heart* and the *beliefs* held there. This is well supported by the context of the Psalms of David that we have recently quoted. So, when this area is out of order, not whole, or not as God intended, it means problems for us.

Broken?
In the Gospel of Luke chapter 4 we see the statement that the Spirit of the Lord is upon Jesus to Heal the Broken Hearted. I think that we have thoroughly dealt with what the heart means, but what does it mean for a heart to be 'broken?' Luke 4:18 speaks to this brokenness as follows:

*"The Spirit of the LORD is upon Me, Because He has anointed Me To preach the gospel to the poor; He has sent Me to heal the **brokenhearted**, To proclaim liberty to the captives"* (NKJV emphasis mine).

If our hearts are our *central beliefs that produce emotions*, then how does that relate to being broken? I think that we can deduce that if our thinking and feelings are not whole or as they were intended to be, then they are broken and need healing/fixing. We have already established that this is done by receiving truth from the Spirit of truth. The Greek word 'suntribo' translated *'broken' literally means broken, crushed, shattered, or bruised.*

If you have a clock and it has a slightly bent hand on it you would call it broken. If it is smashed to pieces you would also consider it to be broken. Whether you are a little bit broken or you are completely shattered, you are still broken because you are not in the working order that the designer intended. You are not whole. The application here is relating to the state of your heart. So, if your beliefs and feelings are in any way not as they were intended to be, then you are broken.

None of us have perfect truth about ourselves, or about how God really feels about us, therefore we are ALL broken hearted. The only question is how broken, and where are we in the process of sanctification and healing? Now we can see clearly why God desires truth in our hearts. It relates directly to our journey into wholeness and freedom from captivity in every area of our lives.

Many people have had their self-image *broken* down through negative statements and constant criticism. Others are *crushed* under the burden of expectations to perform and please others. Some have had their lives *shattered* through such traumas as physical or sexual abuse. Still more have had their sense of well-being *bruised* through anxiety about being loved and valued. All of the beliefs resulting from this treatment and programming, constitute the brokenness of the human person in *the heart*.

The Greek word 'sozo', normally translated as 'saved' on examination carries a much fuller meaning. As well as saved, it includes; *to be healed, to be delivered and to be made whole*. God did not save us for eternity only, He had in mind for us to be transformed and bring Him glory through our lives on Earth. We have seen that as people are made whole and healed of their brokenness, others see the changes. In turn this proves the integrity of God and the promises in His Word.

Implications of a 'Broken Heart' and Captivity for wrong beliefs
Let me outline seven basic problems that assail mankind. I will not address them in detail here but you will see that each of them is directly impacted by what we believe.

1. Spiritual bondage
This relates firstly to remaining unsaved and a slave to the ruler of this world. Our blindness and lack of knowledge regarding our situation keeps us submitted to this spiritual being. Secondly, we often see areas of demonic strongholds as a part of the mechanism of serving or being held in sin. It is often an undiagnosed element and result of giving *ground* and permitting the *strongman goods*. So, giving place to, and co-operating with unholy spiritual entities, is also based on our bad solutions to our problems which stems from our wrong beliefs.

2. Mental soundness
Beliefs producing fear and anxiety are tormenting and can lead to all kinds of *masking* behaviour. The vast majority of mental problems that are observed begin with beliefs at a *heart* level with chemical imbalances being the outworking. It is also true that some people are born mentally handicapped in some way and others have mental impairment through events such as damage from an accident or drug abuse. In the case of belief based mental issues, there will usually be coinciding emotional and physical implications.

3. Emotional peace
If our minds and thoughts are not at peace then our feelings and emotions will also be out of order. You do not simply have an emotion; remember it is a thought coming from a belief first.

4. Relational wellbeing
If you have mental inner thought issues along with emotional damage, your responses will also be out of order in relationships. Typically, your wrong belief-based hurts will react with the faulty inner thoughts of others making it very difficult to have harmonious interactions.

5. Sexuality
We have even found that in order to come together fully in sexual union there are usually beliefs that need to be dealt with first. This can be basic inner thoughts that affect other areas of life such as; "You don't really care about me; what I want is not important!" Other kinds of brokenness stemming from feelings proceeding from sexual abuse commonly need to be rectified.

Another way that sexuality can be out of order is through belief-based gender confusion. Sexual sin such as adultery or fornication usually proceed from emotional issues such as looking for acceptance, so again all of these things as Jesus stated are *heart issues*.

6. Addictive problems and besetting sins
Addictions are usually related to masking behaviour or coping mechanisms for heart based unresolved emotional issues. They are in effect our solution to our pain or anxiety which lay us open to setting up chemical cycles, associations and bondage to habits to cover our feelings.

7. Physical health
Our bodies are the end of the line in terms of our thought life. How you think about yourself and life will have a direct effect on your health in either a positive or negative way. Your body will flag or play out your inner thought life as your physical feelings are the chemical elaboration of the thoughts. It begins as a thought, becomes a feeling, which in terms of your body is a chemical release. We could say then that if your inner and outer thoughts are positive then it will be reflected in your body, hence the mind/body connection. We can say then that in many ways your physical state begins in your thinking and ends in your body.

CHAPTER 11
Physical healing through healing the broken heart

When we have a thought or belief it goes to the part of the brain called the hypothalamus. This part of the brain oversees, amongst other systems, the central nervous system and the endocrine or glandular system. These glands release hormones into our bodies that are involved in many body functions. In terms of your chemical body, hormones make your world go around.

Perhaps this is most easily demonstrated in some basic life activities. If you begin to think about your favourite food, your hypothalamus will begin to perform the relevant functions to get your body ready to eat. You may now find your stomach grumbling as the hormones involved begin to wind up your gastric system. If you think about a sexual encounter your body will release the appropriate hormones to prepare you for the physical act. Men are far more likely to have a rapid response to these thoughts because, according to the scientists, they have on average 20 to 25 times as much of the sex hormone testosterone. So, guys, it is advisable to avoid potential discomfort, by not thinking about sex before you have cleared the appointment with your wife.

So, we can see the fundamental outworking of our thoughts in our bodies through these simple illustrations. A cheerful or happy heart that is content with life and at peace with self and God will release hormones that promote health and well-being. The word of God says,

"A cheerful heart is good medicine, but a crushed spirit dries up the bones" (NIV, Proverbs 17:22).

A heavy heart, loaded down with negative beliefs will produce hormone imbalances which lead to disease. We say that if your mind is not at peace or at *ease*, you are open to *dis-ease* in your physical body.

A bull in a field

As an example of how this can play out in our bodies, let us look at two hormones in the hormonal cascade that affect each other and need to be in balance with each other. One is called cortisol, which is a stress hormone. It has anti-inflammatory properties and helps mediate actions such as blood sugar balances and so on. There are a number of other hormones that we need to function and be healthy that are in turn made from cortisol. There is another hormone on the other side of the cascade known as DHEA (Dehydroepiandrosterone) also from which many other hormones that we need are made. Amongst other things DHEA is implicated in mood and a sense of wellbeing.

Imagine finding yourself in a field with a snorting bull staring you down. Might I suggest that in that moment you do not need to be in a good mood and feel that all is right with the World! You actually need to have a stress response and go into flight fairly quickly. This is typically what happens with such a threat. Hormones that you need to get you out of the situation such as cortisol rise rapidly and hormones that give you a sense of well-being or are not important in the moment diminish. After the situation is resolved these levels go back to normal.

But what if your stress is coming from a fear related to people such as fear of rejection, failure, or performance anxiety to do with the expectations of others? It is very hard to avoid all humans. There are billions of them and invariably you will need to deal with some of them at some point in time. Anxiety issues related to whether you perform to expectations, or receive acceptance or not, are ever present, daily stressors. Hormonally, this means that your chemicals stay out of balance long term, and usually become more exaggerated over time. This is a common phenomenon in a society founded on achievement, conformity to expectations and success in return for value, significance and worth.

So now you have too much of one hormone and not enough of the other as an outworking of your way of life and culture. Normally, over time, the imbalance of these hormone values become more and more exaggerated. Simplistically this is a typical example of the pathways to disease. Each negative emotion will have some kind of unhelpful effect on your physiology.

Scientific statistics

Modern science confirms what the Bible has always stated, that if our soul is functioning well then the outcome will be health. The most recent statistics that I have heard is that around 90% of diseases proceed from emotionally rooted chemical imbalances. I would suggest that possibly the other 10% are to do with our bad solutions to our emotional problems such as drugs, alcohol, excessive food or even at times prescription medication which can carry a considerable number of side effects. I am not sure that we can lay all of our diseases at the feet of cultural issues, such as a high sugar diet as some do. However, these and other substances that we ingest certainly create an environment for disease to prosper and proliferate.

3 John 1:2 says, *"Dear friend, I pray that you may enjoy good health and that all may go well with you, even as your soul is getting along well"* (NIV).

The preceding passage confirms that if our souls, that is our mind, will and emotions, are in good order then our bodies will also be healthy. As we have seen, the state of our souls and physical well-being are directly linked to the condition and beliefs of our heart. In practice we have seen this to be the case over and over again. If our thought life is conformed to the word of God, both at the voluntary conscious level and also in the heart, we can expect the result to be health. Proverbs 4:20-23 puts it this way,

*"[20] Pay attention, my child, to what I say. Listen carefully. [21] Don't lose sight of my words. Let them penetrate **deep within your heart** [22] for they bring life and **radiant health** to anyone who discovers their meaning. [23] Above all else, guard **your heart**, for it affects everything you do"* (NLT, emphasis mine).

I have read somewhere that there is an area of modern medicine known as bio psychiatry. The premise of this model is that if they could get people to think correctly then nobody would be sick. The concept is correct, however without the power and ministry of the Holy Spirit I suggest that it is impossible for them to attain.

The New King James version translates this passage as the 'issues of life' that come from the heart. Health is certainly an issue that many have to deal with.

"*[20] My son, give attention to my words; Incline your ear to my sayings. [21] Do not let them depart from your eyes; Keep them in the midst of your heart; [22] For they are life to those who find them, And **health to all their flesh**. [23] Keep your **heart** with all diligence, For out of it **spring the issues of life**"* (NKJV, Proverbs 4:20-23 emphasis mine).

The example of a thyroid gland healed

A young lady in her mid-20s came for ministry with a presenting problem of her thyroid counts being, as she put it, *off the charts*. Her doctor was going to start her on hormone treatment immediately. I suggested that we work on the anxiety beliefs that she held that were producing the problem. We spent about an hour investigating and ministering to her anxieties. The next week she returned to her doctor reporting that she was well. His response to the blood test that followed was; *that can't be right, it is all in balance*. And so, he ordered another test which also proved to be perfect. An unexpected bonus from the ministry time was that she reported delightedly, that *the best part was that she didn't have a panic attack*, as she normally would when they did the blood test. Even her anxieties about the blood test were belief based.

A Broken Heart healed, leading to release from a physical malady

A number of years ago we were ministering in a large church in a rural city in Australia. A lady in her 50s was on the list to come for help and she was suffering from a variety of emotional problems. She was very eager to be set free and so her session went unusually quickly. Most of her problems were as a result of a considerable amount of sexual abuse in her early life. After around 45 minutes she reported that she was completely at peace and so we concluded our time together.

About 2 to 3 weeks later I received a message from her reporting all of the many benefits from the session. Unexpectedly she also reported that she no longer had to be hospitalized weekly for treatment to her liver and kidneys. I was not even aware that she had a problem as she had not mentioned it. Consequently, I had not prayed for her healing, it was simply a by-product of her broken heart being healed by the Spirit of Christ.

At times we deliberately target beliefs that produce disease, and other times it happens unbidden as a result of the healing and release from captive thoughts and feelings taking place. We have seen various problems, such as arthritis or asthma, being healed without direct prayer. Somewhere in the process of an emotional release, the body comes back into order and they simply disappear. That is certainly not to say that God does not heal the body in a number of other ways, it is a way that we see God healing the sick.

The power of life and death
Proverbs 18:21, *"The tongue has the power of life and death, and those who love it will eat its fruit"* (NIV).

This proverb suddenly becomes very powerful in its potential power to break a heart. For example, in its simplest form, when a child is told that they are stupid, useless or in some way inadequate, it becomes part of the programming of the identity or self-beliefs within their hearts. The echoes of these beliefs are literally a breeding ground for negative emotions eventually leading to disease and finally premature death. Not only might they impact on the length of life, they will almost certainly have an effect on the quality of life. Fortunately, Jesus promised us that He came to set the captives free in order for us to have abundant life to the full.

If we have been crushed by negative words, it will be difficult to have a cheerful heart that releases healthy hormones. A heavy heart that has been crushed this way will load our human spirit down in its ability to empower our bodies to function properly.

Proverbs 18:14 says, *"A man's spirit sustains him in sickness, but a crushed spirit who can bear?"* (NIV).

The heavy weight of a broken heart will sap away the life-giving function of the human spirit. We have already seen that a crushed or broken spirit dries up the bones. Other authors have already documented that the blood cells making up the immune system are manufactured in the bone marrow. If this is dried out it becomes pretty obvious that this can lead to some pretty serious diseases that have their Etiology or causation in immune cell production or disruption.

Autoimmune disease

Statistics vary, but a general figure of 1 out of every 7 to 10 people in the U.S. suffer from what is termed autoimmune disease. I imagine that the numbers would be similar across the developed World. There are more than 80 of these diseases listed. Some Christian commentators consider the root of the autoimmune component of diseases to be self-rejection, and we have found this to be the case.

Remember your body is the end of the line for your thought life. If, at a heart level you do not accept yourself then, your body will play out those thoughts. In essence you yourself become the enemy of your own acceptability because of some kind of perception that you hold about your worthiness. Your body then follows your thoughts by attacking itself. Some state that your immune system will then attack the weakest link in the chain. If you have stress, fear or anxieties this may be your thyroid or your adrenal glands for example. If you are overweight and your pancreas is overworked you may be a candidate for diabetes. At times we see people who are enormous and massively overweight or morbidly obese but they are not diabetic. They certainly have created an environment for the disease but emotionally they do not hold inner beliefs that make them predisposed.

Everything starts with a thought

I have come to the conclusion that everything begins with a thought that is shaped by what we believe. Further, the beliefs of the heart are most powerful in terms of their implications because we do not usually know what they are or how to rectify them without the Holy Spirit. The outworking's of these range from your own personal inner health and relationships, right through to world leaders with low self-image making decisions based on their emotional needs and beginning world wars. The thoughts of the heart are the principle issue with implications for everything. How we are programmed becomes critical. 1 Corinthians 2:10-11 states,

"[10] *But God has revealed them to us through His Spirit. For the Spirit searches all things, yes, the deep things of God.* [11] *For what man knows the things of a man except the spirit of the man which is in him? Even so no one knows the things of God except the Spirit of God"* (NKJV).

CHAPTER 12
Gods own perspective for those suffering in this area

Before we begin with how to practically work with the Spirit of truth in applying this ministry, let us examine God's position and provision towards this ministry. Do we need to talk God into helping us, or is it His idea?

Do you want more of the presence of God, or anointing on you?

Let us begin with a couple of Old Testament passages firstly encouraging our involvement and commitment to the ministry, and then a prophetic account of what those who respond to these passages will be doing.

Isaiah 57:15 states, *"For this is what the high and lofty One says-- he who lives forever, whose name is holy: "I live in a high and holy place, but also with him who is contrite and lowly in spirit, to revive the **spirit of the lowly** and to **revive the heart** of the contrite"* (NIV, emphasis mine).

We have to 'tease out' the exact meaning from the Hebrew that this passage comes from. He is saying that, He is with the contrite (Heb. Dakka - meaning, crushed or destroyed) and the lowly in spirit (Heb. Shaphal - meaning depressed). He is with them to revive them (Revive Heb. Chayah – meaning, to make alive, quicken, recover, repair, restore (to life), revive, save, to make or be whole).

This is much the same meaning as the NT Greek word 'sozo'. His promise is also to revive their *hearts*, which coming from the Hebrew word *Leb*, as we have pointed out means the feelings, intellect and will. Or perhaps we could suggest the feelings proceeding from our beliefs which affect our choices.

In the New Testament we have words such as 'Anapsuksis' which is normally translated as 'refreshing' but in the Greek it is actually, 'recovery of breath' or 'revival.' So, whatever you think about what 'revival' is, from a Biblical perspective, it is bringing life back to an individual's spirit and heart. A *revival* is when enough people are revived to change a community, city or even a nation.

Acts 3:19 says, "*Repent, then, and turn to God, so that your sins may be wiped out, that times of **refreshing** (Anapsuksis, - recovery of breath, revival) may come from the Lord*" (NIV, emphasis mine).

The basis of this is **repent**. This literally means to 'think differently,' or 'reconsider how you think.' Once we have changed our minds about how we regard God and His kingdom, it falls to Him to revive us and bring us to wholeness. As we know, in Luke chapter 4 and verses 18-19, Jesus unravelled the scroll of Isaiah and quoted from chapter 61 regarding what He was now about to do. However, in Isaiah 61 the chapter goes beyond what Jesus reads and details what those that had received healing of *their* broken hearts and freedom from captivity were going to do. Isaiah 61:1-3 notes that,

"*¹ The Spirit of the Lord GOD is upon Me, because the LORD has anointed me to preach good tidings to the poor; He has sent Me to heal the brokenhearted, to proclaim liberty to the captives, And the opening of the prison to those who are bound; To proclaim the acceptable year of the LORD, and the day of vengeance of our God; ² To comfort all who mourn; ³ to console those who mourn in Zion, to give them beauty for ashes, the oil of joy for mourning, the garment of praise for the spirit of heaviness.*"

Up until this point He is talking about what He, in the first instance, will do for us. Next, He shifts to what the results of this ministry to us will be, and the passage moves on to what we who have received from Him will be doing:

"*³ That **they** may be called trees of righteousness, the planting of the LORD, that He may be glorified. ⁴ And **they** shall rebuild the old ruins, **they** shall raise up the former desolations, and **they** shall repair the ruined cities, The desolations of many generations*" (NKJV, Isaiah 61:3-4, emphasis mine).

I believe that in type, the ruined cities refer to the broken human personality. Jesus referred to His own body as being a temple. The Bible also states that we are the temple of the Holy Spirit. So, the picture of the temple, or a city is not an uncommon portrayal of the human personality in the scriptures. This position is strengthened from other passages which refer to setting yourself on helping people receive the promises, such as Isaiah 58. Another example is that found in Proverbs 25:28.

"Like a city whose walls are broken down is a man who lacks self-control" (NIV).

This passage refers to the ability of a man to resist and defend his person from participating with outside spiritual pressure. For example, normal emotional control being compromised through drugs or alcohol abuse.

As we round out our thoughts on the subject of Truth Encounters from a Biblical perspective, we can be encouraged to note in the following passage some powerful promises for our own healings as we set and position ourselves to free others. My wife and I can confirm that God is faithful to His word. We have progressively received healing and freedom ourselves as we have dedicated our lives to ministering to others.

Isaiah 58:6-12, *"⁶ Is not this the kind of fasting I have chosen: to loose the chains of injustice and untie the cords of the yoke, to set the oppressed free and break every yoke? ⁷ Is it not to share your food with the hungry and to provide the poor wanderer with shelter-- when you see the naked, to clothe him, and not to turn away from your own flesh and blood? ⁸ **Then your light will break forth like the dawn, and your healing will quickly appear;** then your righteousness will go before you, **and the glory of the LORD will be your rear guard**. ⁹ Then you will call, and the LORD will answer; you will cry for help, and he will say: Here am I. "If you do away with the yoke of oppression, with the pointing finger and malicious talk, ¹⁰ **and if you spend yourselves in behalf of the hungry and satisfy the needs of the oppressed, then your light will rise in the darkness, and your night will become like the noonday**. ¹¹ The LORD will guide you always; he will satisfy your needs in a sun-scorched land and will strengthen your frame. You will be like a well-watered garden, like a spring whose waters never fail. ¹² Your people will rebuild the ancient ruins and will raise up the age-old foundations; **you will be called Repairer of Broken Walls**, Restorer of Streets with Dwellings".*

It is clear in the New Testament that Jesus discipled His followers into doing what He did. The Father's Will shall always involve ministering to, or supporting, those who are helping people to receive salvation, healing and freedom. If the Father is all about meeting the needs of the people He created, then it is inevitable that His children will be dedicated to the same activities.

PART 2

RECEIVING YOUR FREEDOM THROUGH A TRUTH ENCOUNTER

- You Will Indeed Be Set Free -

CHAPTER 13
Accessing the Heart via the mind and emotions

Screens, icons, programs

For the sake of an illustration, let us imagine your conscious mind as a screen; perhaps as a television (TV) screen. In today's world there can often be up to 100 channels or more on our TV. On a normal TV set you can only view one channel or program at a time. We described in Chapter 7 how in much the same way, if I begin to talk about a hot dog or your favourite meal you may now have a picture on the screen of your mind. To access that picture of food you had to put whatever else you were thinking about to the side and change channels briefly. Your conscious mind is much like a computer in this respect, having been designed to be a sequential processor, or in other words to focus on one task at a time.

In a ministry session then, we are tuning into the fear, rejection or whatever other channel in order to view and connect with it. Thinking now of a hot dog, if we focus on it long enough, we will begin to have something happen in our stomachs as a reaction to the thought. In the same way as we begin to concentrate on, and embrace our fear or other issues, bringing them onto the screen of our conscious minds, we will have a chemical bodily response that we call emotion or feelings.

We can now begin to look for the belief and inner thoughts producing the emotion. Whether we present with a negative emotion and identify the belief producing it, or have a negative belief and let ourselves feel it, is immaterial. The important thing is that we connect them both on the conscious screen of our minds. Usually people will come presenting with negative emotions such as anxiety, fear, anger, rejection, bitterness and so on. Some people will look for help because of how they are reacting in relationships or to life.

As you listen to their story or problem you will most likely hear the beliefs behind the emotions come out in words. I usually have a piece of paper or a notebook with me, and record statements that I believe may be connected to beliefs. Jesus said that we will hear the overflow of the heart from the mouth: Matthew 12:34b states,

"... for out of the overflow of the **heart** the **mouth** speaks." (NIV, emphasis mine).

For example, in the course of telling their story, somebody might say something such as; 'school was a difficult time for me, but that's not surprising, I can never keep up with the other kids!' When the time comes for ministry, we could say to them something along the lines of, 'I heard you say before that you can never keep up with the other kids; is that true?' Now, as they concentrate on that statement and connect with the feeling that goes with it, we can ask a further question to find out the belief of the heart. 'What does that make you if you can't keep up with the other kids?' Their possible answer may be something such as; 'I must be dumb!'

The next thing that we want to do is find the place where they first learned this; the critical moment when they 'took it to heart.' There is always a historically matching memory. They may report something along the lines of, 'when I was in grade 3, I could not do my times table and the teacher embarrassed me in front of the class.' So, I would probably say something along the lines of, 'so in that moment you believed that you **are** dumb because you could not do the times table?' Response 'Yes.'

Then I would say something such as, 'Lord, Fred believes that he is dumb and can't keep up with other people because he could not do his times table. His truth is that *he is dumb*; what is your truth for him?' As 'Fred' now has the belief, the matching negative feeling, and the historical event pulled up onto the screen of his mind it is time to ask God to reveal *His* truth to set him free. Whatever, God does in that moment will set 'Fred' free simply because He is God. The key for *us* in helping Fred is finding what is believed in his heart.

We tend to remember whatever is stored in the moment of emotional weakness and vulnerability. Surrounding details are not necessarily a part of interpreting the event so much as what is happening in the moment. God could remind him that he had been off sick and was not present when the instruction to learn those times tables was given.

Remember, this whole event including beliefs were beneath the surface in the heart all along. They needed to be deliberately accessed and brought into the conscious mind to be processed. It is necessary to know what you believe before you can present it to the Lord to address it with His truth.

Dealing with multiple beliefs

Rounding out our illustration of a television screen, let us consider the multiple channels again. When we first began this ministry, people would come to us for help, and in a session, we might work through 2 or 3 beliefs and feelings that were a problem. They would usually report how free they felt, and we would be thinking that we had just worked with the Lord to fix up their whole lives! In some cases, people were happy with their new freedom, but many times we would be contacted with a report that they were struggling again. Upon investigation we would find out that everything resolved in the previous session was still settled, but there were other new issues. We have found this to be the case in ministering to others as well as receiving healing for ourselves. Most of us have a significant number of *channels* that need to be *reprogrammed*.

By way of example, someone may come presenting a problem of fear. They may have a fear of rejection, failure, flying, abandonment, or lack of protection or provision and so on. Each of these fears is a different belief and stem from various historical events. You can only have one of these *channels or programs* running in your conscious mind at a time. It is necessary to go through them one at a time and switch them off individually, so to speak. You only need one fear program still running to feel, for example, anxiety. Typically, as you go through ministering to each belief the intensity becomes less and less until they are completely free.

That is not to suggest that every fear needs to be dealt with before your anxiety is completely gone. It is usually fear related to people that is ever present, such as fear of rejection. It is difficult to not deal with people as there are billions of them on the Earth. A fear of flying, for example, may produce no anxiety at all because you simply choose not to fly. However, if you have to fly for some reason, your belief-based anxiety will quickly be present and need to be resolved.

The 'Golf' principle

I once saw a picture of the famous golfer Tiger Woods standing beside a pile of golf balls that would fill a shopping trolley. He was basically practicing producing the same swing over and over. The courses may change, the competition varies, the conditions will be different, but he is doing the same thing over and over. In much the same way we have a handful of questions that we use over and over to help people identify that which they believe. Sometimes we will be visiting fear channels, other times switching of all of the rejection or bitterness channels. On occasions we will be finding the beliefs behind sin.

Some people will be very emotionally connected and receive the ministry easily. Others will have defences and objections or be people who want to resolve their own problems with their minds and have not been able to. Whatever comes to us, as co laborers with the Holy Spirit, we patiently and graciously give our time, repetitively, asking the same handful of questions!

After a while, once you become familiar with the process you will find yourself ministering a *truth encounter* driving with someone in a car, across a table at lunch, in a prayer line or more purposefully in a prayer room at some location. The point is that once you learn the simple process you will be applying it over and over to different cases. It is very rewarding to see God setting people free, and Him allowing us the privilege of being involved.

'Icons' and 'shortcuts'
Before we move on, I want to push out the parameters of the *screen* in the conscious mind analogy. Up to this point, we have discussed it as a television screen in order to illustrate that some people may have many *channels and programs* that need to be worked through, and others just a few. It doesn't actually reflect on you as a person how many negative beliefs that you have collected. It is a bit like being clothed by life. Someone's clothing may be expensive and plentiful; another's may be dirty and tattered. In the end we are all the same, just people clothed by different circumstances and conditions.

We know that God looks at who you are and not the outer appearance, this includes weighing justly your circumstances and how you arrived where you are. We cannot then judge anyone's behaviour in any way. Something happened to produce the responses, everyone has a story, and if nothing negative happened to you then you can consider yourself blessed. You need to know though, that if you were the product of the same situations, then you would probably hold the same beliefs and produce the same attitudes and behaviour. These responses to beliefs I call, universal reactions. They are predictable reactions to beliefs that are held. I will illustrate these in a later chapter.

Computer screens

Most people today have seen a computer screen. We can use this as an analogy to further examine how our conscious mind operates. On most screens are little pictures called icons which have some kind of symbol depicting the program that they represent. The program is in the unit stored in a deeper place. On my computers you have to click a button twice with the pointer on the icon to open the program.

The point is that these icons connect you to programs that are there underneath whether you open them or not. In the case of operating the computer most of these are opened as a deliberate act. This can be the case with our minds. For example, we can purposefully open the *time to cook the dinner* program which holds all the information that we have stored and held as data about preparing food. It will come up onto our screen and we will access what we know to complete the task. In my case all there is when I open the *prepare dinner program* is, *'buy Pizza'*.

Associations

With regard to our minds, these programs are often accessed by situations or circumstances automatically. We call these *associations*. Perhaps the simplest way to explain this would be something like the ringing of your telephone. Your brain associates the sound with somebody wanting to talk to you. It then opens the *program* containing information on how to answer the phone and most likely selects the most suitable response, depending on whether you expect it to be a friend or a grumpy employer.

Emotionally, we operate along much the same lines. Perhaps we are starting a new job in a crowded office. Without deliberately wanting to, we access an anxiety belief. Stored in the memory in the file along with the belief is *how do I react in this situation?* The belief could be something like, *people won't like me unless I do what they want and make them happy,* and this has been learnt from a historical event. The response to the situation, also stored in the memory, could be something such as, to entertain them and be funny. This may have been how they gained acceptance and fitted in as a child in similar situations. So, the behaviour coming from the *I need to perform to be accepted belief* is a mask.

People often present with these types of situations on their *shopping lists* for healing. They would most likely come into a session reporting anxiety in these environments. We have them *click on* the *I am uncomfortable in group situations* icon on the screen of their conscious minds. By that I mean, concentrate on this type of situation and how it makes them feel. Then, we identify a matching historical event with the same emotions in it and clarify what is believed that produces the feelings. Once we have these elements, we can invite the Spirit of truth to minister freedom to them.

Shortcuts
Before we move on from the screen analogy, I would like to point out that these icons are readily accessible shortcuts to the programs within the computer that bypass the normal pathways. This is a helpful picture for us in terms of resolving habitual sin cycles. Let us create a common scenario.

A married woman struggles with rejection having never had true love and acceptance in childhood. As a consequence, deep inside she believes that she is *not loveable or good enough to be noticed.* The spouse, because of their own issues, is always at work, playing golf or at the pub with his friends. He feels that he has shown love by getting her a nice house and a car. Along the way she meets a nice man at work who comments on her hair. Later he invites her for a coffee.

Up until this point the whole process is going through the normal pathways of feeling that this is wrong, knowing that you shouldn't be doing it, but at the same time, mistaking the good feeling of being cared about as love. Usually your emotional needs will be the greatest predictor of your behaviour and eventually she moves past the self-conflict into an illicit relationship. After the first time, the person no longer works through the normal pathways regarding whether or not the sin should be entered into. Now this is the apparent solution to their rejection and they *shortcut* the process and go straight to the sinful activity. Without being set free from the underlying rejection beliefs, she can easily fall into further affairs. Typically, with both men and women, when their rejection is resolved they struggle to see how they could have gotten into the situation to begin with.

Another example could be a man addicted to pornography. At one time he felt convicted and guilty. But eventually when the opportunity or situation presents for him to access the sin, it is now a shortcut and he goes directly to the sin without inner opposition. His heart is hardened and he no longer goes through any thinking process that would hold resistance or objection, he goes directly to the sin.

2 Peter 2:19b says, *"for a man is a slave to whatever has mastered him"* (NIV).

Many sins have an emotional need component as the original trigger which needs to be resolved. Christians are not any different to anyone else in terms of their humanity and emotional needs. They are not the same as other people, however, in that they have the opportunity to be set free.

In summary then, as a tool to help our understanding, we know that when people look to us to connect them to God for healing, we need to get them to go through the exercise of connecting, consciously and deliberately, with information that they hold in their hearts. Some are hesitant to do that and you may need to spend some time working through getting them to look at the problem and bring it up onto the *screen* of their conscious mind. Quiet rooms and a one on one session are ideal for this where possible. If they are prepared to, I have them focus on their thoughts or feelings, and go to what I term *periscope depth*. This is where they begin to concentrate on, and explore, what is underneath in the heart.

Note:
We can only minister to whatever a person is wanting help with. It is entirely up to them. God will not make them get ministry and neither should we. Our job is to offer healing if they desire it. We can encourage people to work through everything that they can

find. Some people will, for example, be pleased to get rid of a fear or the like, but are happy to keep their pride and rebellion. It's almost as if they go, 'thanks for that God, but I am taking over again and am satisfied with my own solutions!' This is between God and the person; it is not our place to judge, only to be equipped to help when possible. We can only work with whatever issue that they present with.

CHAPTER 14
Sources of & Influences on Heart beliefs

The Generational principle
Exodus 20: 5-6, states, "⁵ *For I, the LORD your God, am a jealous God, **visiting the iniquity of the fathers on the children** to the third and fourth generations of those who hate Me,* ⁶ *but showing mercy **to thousands**, to those who love Me and keep My commandments*" (NKJV).

Doing the mathematics, Almighty God offers mercy to one thousand generations for those who show their love by keeping His commandments. That is 250 to 333 times more that He wants us to be blessed; than He wants us to be disciplined! If there are no consequences then there is no fear of God. However, this passage makes it abundantly clear that He wants to encourage us and reward us for showing our love for Him. God's love language is obedience.

John 14:15, "*If you love Me, keep My commandments*" (NKJV).
John 14:15, "*If you love me, you will obey what I command*" (NIV).

The *visiting* in Exodus 20:5 is like a *drawing to*. On face value, it almost seems as if the father's sin in a particular area, becomes an area where the children will be tested to see if they love God and prefer His commandments and ways. Will they seek Him to be free from their sins and weaknesses?

Have you ever wondered why, in a neighbourhood, some of the residents are alcoholics, while others will never have a drink in their lives but are drawn like a magnet to horror movies, drugs, violence or pornography? This is the outworking of the *visiting* on the family line. Under the curse of the law this was the consequence of iniquity. It continues today for those who remain under the judgment of the law, not having believed that Jesus fulfilled the law and took the penalty of the curse in their place. Sin is defined by the law, it did not begin with the law; it began with Satan and entered the human generation line through Adam and Eve.

Positions on generational principles
Let me give you three distorted positions that Christians often hold pertaining to generational principles:

1. It was 'all done at the cross.'
This doctrine proposes that Jesus ended the penalty of the curse and so there are now no effects on Christians. This is a *positionally* true statement. Jesus did pay for our freedom from the curse of the law; hence all of His part was *done at the cross*. But we need to know that all of these promises are under the New Covenant which is mediated and accessed by faith. In the event that this were automatic and operative without the faith component there would be no sick Christians, no mental, emotional, relational issues or sin addictions to be dealt with. It is reasonably obvious that this is not the case. All of these maladies one way or another relate to the curse of sin through our generations all the way back to Adam.

The truth remains though, that Jesus did pay for the curse that passes through the generation lines, and largely we appropriate that provision of freedom through the ministries of the Holy Spirit. Water baptism is an ideal time to pray against dynamics coming through the family, as you are choosing to put the old life behind. We have seen evidence such as repeated accidents as a result of a family curse stop when we have prayed specifically against them at water baptism. But again, you will only be able to access by faith those things that you are aware of. As a consequence, many other areas are discerned later in further ministry settings.

Galatians 3:13, "*Christ redeemed us from the curse of the law by becoming a curse for us, for it is written: 'Cursed is everyone who is hung on a tree'*" (NIV).

Still others believe that traits passing from generation to generation simply do not exist. In a practical sense, observing even our physical characteristics and mannerisms and those of our parents and ancestors quickly dispels this thought. Even practices such as architecture or diet have a generational influence.

2. All of your healing and freedom will come through dealing with generational issues.
This group has you renouncing everything that you can possibly think of. Personally, I have not seen freedom come to many people

using this model. If your generational influences have become your personal sin then you need to confess, repent and be ministered to and set free. It can become an excessive practice that is meaningless. I have seen people with issues that could be easily ministered to endlessly and fervently going through books renouncing all kinds of sins of their ancestors.

The truth is that Jesus DID take the penalty of that curse for you. Now by faith and through the ministry of the Holy Spirit you can be set free. Self-effort in renouncing will not yield much without Him. A minister led by the Spirit may help you with the prayer of faith in these times. In the Old Testament we see that Balaam could not curse the people of God as they were protected. The method that was used to expose them and bring a curse on them was by getting them to participate in the sins of the societies around them.

3. The children eat sour grapes.
In arguing that generational influences are not relevant to Christians, people often quote the book of the major prophet Ezekiel in order to imply that generational principles are no longer in effect.

Ezekiel 18:1-3, "*The word of the LORD came to me again, saying;* [2] "*What do you mean when you use this proverb concerning the land of Israel, saying: 'The fathers have eaten sour grapes, And the children's teeth are set on edge'?* [3] "*As I live," says the Lord GOD, "you shall no longer use this proverb in Israel".*

If these people were to look further to the same account in the book of Jeremiah they would see a fuller explanation of this. Remember, they are both prophetic books speaking of a time to come.

Jeremiah 31: 29-34, [29] "*In those days they shall say no more:* **'The fathers have eaten sour grapes, And the children's teeth are set on edge.'** [30] "*But every one shall die for his own iniquity; every man who eats the sour grapes, his teeth shall be set on edge.* [31] "*Behold, the days are coming, says the LORD, when I will* **make a new covenant** *with the house of Israel and with the house of Judah;* [32] "*not according to the covenant that I made with their fathers in the day that I took them by the hand to lead them out of the land of Egypt, My covenant which they broke, though I was a husband to them, says the LORD.* [33] **"But this is the covenant that I will make with the house of Israel** *after those days, says the LORD: I will put My law in their minds, and write it on their hearts; and I will be their God, and they shall be My people.* ³⁴ "No more shall every man teach his neighbor, and every man his brother, saying, 'Know the LORD,' for they all shall know Me, from the least of them to the greatest of them, says the LORD. **For I will forgive their iniquity, and their sin I will remember no more"** (NKJV, Emphasis mine).

Clearly, the expanded Jeremiah passage refers to the new covenant of provision through faith which was established for us by Jesus. You will find this in the book of Hebrews Chapter 10 in the New Covenant directly quoting Jeremiah. (See previous and following underlined passages). So, we can deduce that the prophetic biblical statement that was made by Jeremiah and Ezekiel regarding 'sour grapes' referred to the covenant that we are now under. It was not something for their times.

Hebrews 10:16-17 **"This is the covenant that I will make with them after those days, says the LORD: I will put My laws into their hearts, and in their minds I will write them,"** ¹⁷ then He adds, **"Their sins and their lawless deeds I will remember no more"** (NKJV Emphasis mine. The same as Jeremiah 31:33-34).

How then should we regard generational principles?
As we have already established, Jesus paid the price for our freedom from generational influences. We consider co-labouring with the ministry of the Holy Spirit as a part of facilitating that freedom in a person's life. Because Jesus has already paid for their release then we can now simply consider generational influences as another potential source for their problem.

Let me give a very simple example of this. Imagine a parent has suffered from rejection from their own family. Remember the nature of God is always accepting. God did not reject man, man rejected God. Rejection then, not being one of the ways of God, can be considered as iniquitous or fundamentally, a sin-based activity. In this simple illustration then we see that the parents sinned against the child in not accepting them. Almost certainly they also suffered areas of rejection from their generations. Our sample parent then, having not received acceptance for their person will most likely continue the cycle, Christian or not, until it is broken.

Are we then getting them to renounce rejection when they come for help? No, we don't even necessarily need to know that it is generational. We are simply ministering to the beliefs that are now held as a result of the rejection. Now, as they have acceptance themselves on the inside, the cycle is broken and they will be carriers of love and grace. Their children may also need some ministry if they have already been affected by the rejection.

When we are dealing with emotional and heart-based healing, regardless of the source the ministry is the same, although we may observe that the source is generational. The ministry is actually appropriating the freedom from the curse that was promised under the New Covenant.

Deliverance from generationally transmitted weaknesses
Although not directly related to our 'Truth Encounters' subject, I will mention here that at times, deliverance of an evil spirit can go along with the ministry. A number of years ago I was ministering to an elderly lady who had suffered with guilt from an event early in her life. She eventually confessed that she had performed a sexual act with a dog. As well as ministry to the beliefs that she held relating to the event, she was delivered from a generational spirit drawing her to the bestiality act. She had never confessed this episode to another person prior to seeing me.

A few years later her middle-aged daughter also came for emotional healing. Towards the end of the session she confessed something that she had never told anyone before. When she was a young girl, she had also had sex with a dog. She also needed deliverance from the unclean spirit compelling her to this act.

Once you have seen a few of these cases there are no further doubts regarding generational influences. They were both lovely people, and both exemplary Christians, but there was an area of weakness that had come to them that they had not chosen.

Over the years we have seen many people set free from influences which cause them great guilt and condemnation. They are so relieved to realize that they are not inherently evil people, but something happened in their generations further upstream that they did not ask for. Their specific area of *visiting* was not something that they had read about in the will!

Hereditary disease

If you attend doctors for some kind of chronic illness or disease, they will usually ask you if it is in the family. Physiologically they may test and observe some kind of genetic predisposition for the onset of the disease. We have already previously discussed studies that propose that as many as 90% of diseases stem from emotional imbalances.

I would like to suggest, and have noted over many years, that what actually passes through families are particular emotional problems that create an environment for that specific malady. For example, hereditary self-rejection will give opportunity for autoimmune problems to proliferate in a family line. So, dealing with rejection which has led to self-rejection will remove the predisposition for further generations to suffer. I have observed other troubles such as bitterness and resentment in families that suffer from illnesses such as cancer and arthritis. For the glorious Church that will shine in these dark times, disease prevention may well be just as important as cure.

Epigenetics and secular science

Incidentally, modern secular science confirms the biblical generational principle. Most of that which the modern world is discovering relating to people can be found in your Bible which was written thousands of years ago by the creator of everything! It is already well documented that disease can be hereditary or generational. Epigenetics is an area of science that is stating that habits, behaviour and addictions, for example, are also transmitted through the family.

The following statement is quoted from an article on Epigenetics that I was sent. The passage is from a Neuropsychologist, where Dr. Timothy Jennings explains:

The choices we make – the foods that we eat, the things that we watch – can affect how DNA is expressed. When we have kids, we pass on the sequence to them. So, if we become addicted to stuff, we can pass along to our children gene instructions that make them more vulnerable to addictions. So, take pornography addiction, for instance, since it's the fastest growing epidemic in today's church.

According to a recent study, 68% of Christian men are addicted to porn. Most likely, they are unaware of the hereditary ramifications of viewing porn. It doesn't happen generally with one exposure to pornography. It's the repetitive volitional exposure to pornography that will cause this type of gene expression change to happen".
*Dr. Jennings has a U-Tube series explaining Neuroplasticity and Epigenetics

In practice, we have usually found that the parents of men addicted to porn have also had the problem. Christians are not exempt from these principles and temptations in the World, but we do have the option of freedom. This is just one example. We acknowledge that whether we are dealing with beliefs that need truth, or sin problems that need deliverance or other ministry, generational sources are something that we need to be aware of.

Conception
Our next source is at conception. We have just discussed how dispositions towards beliefs, physical predispositions, behaviour and even habits can pass to us, generationally and spiritually. This would pass to us at conception. It is well documented that the point of life beginning is as the sperm meets the egg and that there is at that moment a little *fireworks* display. For many Christians we would accept this to be the time where the human spirit and soul were placed within that first single fertilized cell. The scientists tell us that this flash of light is the moment when life begins.

We thank our mothers and fathers for joining with God in creation in providing our chemical bodies. But indeed, our spirits and souls are created by our Father in Heaven, who purposed us for Himself to spend eternity with Him. However, we are looking at the challenges we face that hinder our fruitfulness on the journey as we prepare for that time.

Transference at conception
In the following passage, King David ties his weakness and subsequent iniquity with Bathsheba to sinfulness that he received right at conception. Notably, in Psalm 51, verse six, he cites the solution and best defence against self-deception and sin as being truth in the inner parts, or heart as some translations render it.

Psalm 51:5-7, "⁵ *Surely I was sinful at birth, **sinful from the time my mother conceived me**. ⁶ Surely you desire **truth in the inner parts**; you teach me wisdom in the inmost place.⁷ Cleanse me with hyssop, and I will be clean; wash me, and I will be whiter than snow*" (NIV, Emphasis mine).

Many years ago, we were traveling interstate between cities. I was asked by a person that I knew if we would be prepared to minister to a relative of theirs as we passed through their city. On the way to the home of the subject I did a little research on the internet regarding their disease. They were suffering from an unusual heart disease, and according to the medical information that I read on the internet it began at *conception*. This amazed me that medical Etiology of the disease stated that it began at the time of a couple of cells receiving life. There is no heart, so how physically can heart disease begin here if you are basing your study on physiology and scientific evidence and not spiritual concepts?

It turned out that, as is the case with many forms of heart disease, fear was at the root. In this case, fear of death was the problem, which could indeed, be passed at conception. The Lord gave the person a picture which they reported as resolving the fear that was received at conception.

As a source, I will not spend much time on conception as it is relatively unusual for a belief to be birthed right in that moment. However, it is good to be aware of the possibility. None of these sources of beginnings are places that you deliberately look for or suggest. It will usually come from the person that you are working with.

Let me offer this story to illustrate what I am saying. Please note again that it is a fairly rare occurrence, which has presented on a few occasions in more than 20 years of facilitating this kind of ministry. I would hate to spark off a group of people targeting ministry to *conception* as Christians tend to do.

Important note:
People seem to love; 'this is how you do it' models. This is the exact opposite of how this ministry works. We are not directive at all as

to where the ministry should go. But as we explore what people are 'feeling and believing,' as the beginning point, with the direction of the Holy Spirit we *discover* the source.

A young lady was presenting with a feeling of defilement and a sense of being unclean. As we asked her questions and explored her history, we could find no event that would cause her to feel that way. An impression came into her mind of her father forcing himself on her mother in rape. The source of the defilement and uncleanness having been revealed she was subsequently set completely free. As I have stated, this is a very rare and unusual case, and would certainly discourage anyone from suggesting this as a source to anybody that you are helping. If it is something that you need to know, the Holy Spirit will reveal it most likely to the person.

Prenatal, 'before birth'
I have digressed a little here and there but we are looking to find the beliefs that we hold in our hearts that are not God's truth or perspective. In the case of taking in beliefs *prenatal* or while we are still in our mother's womb, we need to realize that these beliefs were initially feelings. Later, when we have words, we can describe the feelings with words. The words are a verbal explanatory version of the feelings or emotions and are one and the same. There is a great deal of science and evidence that indeed a child is impacted by that which both the mother and father are thinking and doing whilst the child is still in the womb [1].

We see instances in the Bible, such as John the Baptist, leaping in the womb when Mary was visiting, carrying the unborn Jesus.

Luke 1:41 says, *"And it happened, when Elizabeth heard the greeting of Mary, that the babe leaped in her womb; and Elizabeth was filled with the Holy Spirit"* (NKJV).

This is an area that you may commonly find yourself ministering in. Again, it is vital that you do not suggest this as the source. When you have exhausted all other possibilities of where beliefs may have begun, and there are no memories then this is a *possible* source.

---

[1] For further study: The Secret Life of the Unborn Child by Thomas Verny M.D. with John Kelly.

Note:
Many people who do not immediately have memories may have suppressed them over time because they are too painful or fearful. There are other reasons for not immediately being able to access memory which we will discuss in a later chapter.

A feeling of not being wanted in a prenatal setting may later be described in words as the belief that no one wants you or perhaps that you are unacceptable. Put simply, rejection is non-acceptance. I have noted, over the years, some predictable beliefs emerging when a child is not accepted when they are known by the parents to be present: 'I don't belong, I am an intruder, I shouldn't be here, I am not wanted, I am not loved...'

There of course can be other reasons coming from memories and events that can cause you to hold those same beliefs. I reiterate that it is vital to not try to take people to a source that you believe may be the root. Just begin with the presenting problem and work backwards into their inner reality.

For example, we have all seen people who come into church, are warmly accepted, loved and valued. Eventually they find a reason to move on, and so they go to many churches, finally, sadly often leaving church altogether. Many times, the reason is, that no matter how much love that they receive, if they hold a belief in their hearts that they *do not belong, are not an accepted part of the group, not really loved, wanted or valued,* they will eventually leave.

All of these beliefs promote anxiety for them in the form of fear of rejection. Once having been rejected, we fear it happening again. This is the most common kind of fear and anxiety, fear of man.

Other kinds of beliefs from prenatal influences
It is very much the case that we can receive any kind of belief that the mother is feeling. If a father has left the mother because he found out that she was pregnant, she will most likely feel she is not important or valued. The child may grow up believing that men will not be there for them and that they do not value you or treat you as important or valuable. This is likely to be a possible root to behaviour such as extreme self-importance and is behind issues

such as narcissistic attitudes. There can, of course, be other events in childhood where these same beliefs have taken hold. A mother, who already has small children and is struggling to manage in some way, may produce a child who has imbibed the mothers' anxious feelings and goes through life stressed from a belief that they will not be able to cope.

An example of how specific situations produce matching beliefs
I teach on prenatal beginnings in our School of Healing and Freedom, and a number of years ago there was a young lady in her mid-twenties attending the sessions. When I began explaining this area, she reported to me later that in her mind she thought to herself, *As if Steve!* The next morning, she was booked in for a ministry session and she was set free from some fears and different problems coming from her memories. Eventually we came to a belief that we discovered began when her mother found out that she was pregnant with her. The situation that she wanted help with was that she had always felt excessively responsible for her mother's life and happiness. Now in her mid-twenties their relationship was such that the daughter's role was that of mother, and the mother looked to the daughter to resolve her problems. The mother even rang up during the ministry session for advice.

As the young lady focused on the feeling of being responsible, and I asked some questions to refine the emotion and belief, the situation unfolded. She remembered her mother, who was 17 years old at the time of discovering the pregnancy, once saying to the unborn child something along the lines of, *you've ruined my life.* For mum, it was the end of being able to do whatever she wanted and she wasn't prepared. The child now believed that she was responsible for the mothers' happiness and it played out in life and their relationship. When God brought perspective, she was greatly relieved to be free of the burden, and promptly booked her mother in for a ministry session for her issues as well!

The point is that we can be very vulnerable to the thoughts and feelings of our parents in the prenatal setting. I could write for some time stories such as people with fear of water that were at Sea in storms in a prenatal event and numerous other situations that are the basis of a person's troubles.

People are going to receive freedom in different ways in their healing moments as God touches them and sets them free. I recall one lady suffering from prenatal rejection reporting something like a warm blue star touching her heart as she felt the pain emanating from her lack of acceptance.

Keeping it simple
Whether prenatal or from another source, you can make an educated guess as to what a person may have been thinking in a given situation or circumstance. As an example, it is common to find a child that has, for instance, been abandoned by the Father either before birth or in early childhood now holding a fear of abandonment. Beliefs such as, *there is no one there for me, there is no one there to protect or provide for me, men don't think I am important,* or other predictable beliefs are common. Once abandoned, insecurity will be a large part of their life, and having been abandoned then the fear of it happening again will be a prominent anxiety. People with these kinds of wounds will typically be controlling and possessive around relationships, often needing constant reassurance that those around them will be there for them. So, it begins in the mind with a fear of abandonment belief such as, *I could be left alone*, and ends in the body with physical problems such as Asthma.

Adopted children may have beliefs such as *where is everybody (familiar) gone? There is no one there for me.*' (That should be there). This can create a considerable amount of fear, anxiety, and even depression.

Helping locate a person close to their beliefs
So as ministers, in our efforts to help we can look at a situation or circumstances, make an educated guess and propose what might be believed, and offer it as a suggestion. This could come out in a statement from you, for instance in a situation where it is known that parents decided not to keep you, as, *So, do you feel like you are not wanted?* People actually know what they feel if they are honest. They will either say *yes I do, no, not really,* or *that's close, but it is more like this or this!* You have simply landed them near their belief. Before you invite the Lord to bring truth there, you might ask a further question such as; *do you feel that there is any reason that you were not wanted?* They may reply that they just feel like they were not wanted, and that is the belief that they hold, or they may respond

with something along the lines of *I feel as though I was not wanted because I was in the way,* or some other kind of qualifying belief.

Note:
If a child is rejected pre-birth, or even after birth and they are feeling not wanted, then even though the parents might change their mind and accept the child later, or perhaps decide to stay together, the child will still have already received the rejection in that moment of emotional breach.

Whatever the source, the thoughts and beliefs that have been encoded in the heart will match that which you would reasonably expect to be taken in given the content of the event.

Note regarding suggesting possible beliefs
Some ministries doing this kind of work would never suggest a possible belief. Their guidelines could be something such as that the person must discover the belief themselves. I could never see any practical reason for this. People come to you to help them identify whatever it is that they believe is causing their problem. Basing your suggestions on what you would expect could be reasonably taken in as a belief can make a session dramatically shorter, which leaves you more time to minister into other areas. I have never seen anyone agree with a suggested belief to please me. They either say, *yes exactly, almost, but it's more like this, or, no, that is not it.*

The more ministry experience that you have, the more discernment and skill you have at helping identify beliefs. Of course, it is not a technique or method that has to be followed. The same results are achieved simply by asking questions. Suggesting belief options is simply a tool that may be appropriate in some situations. It may prove to be helpful with, for example, some subjects who don't quite understand what it is that you are looking for.

Gender confusion with prenatal influences as one potential source
Many times, I have found people who feel that they should have been the opposite gender. This often stems from people wanting the child to be born a particular sex. A few years ago, when I was teaching Pastors on this in Africa, one of the hosts took the platform after I had finished the session. He bravely proclaimed that when his

daughter was in his wife's womb, and given that they had wanted a boy, he prayed and prophesied over the child that it would be a male. Now, he confessed, as a grown-up girl, when he leaves the house she puts on his clothes. It really is best to leave the selection to the creator.

At times I have ministered to some farmer's daughters who illustrate this affect. Their hair is cut like men's hair, they wear men's overalls, and they can often outwork the men on the farm. It is not uncommon for them to also exhibit lesbian tendencies. The farmers have wanted boys to help with the farm work and so these girls have felt from before birth which position in the family that they should fulfil. Remember, as a principle, *as a person thinks in their heart so are they!* (Proverbs 23:7). These girls think in their *hearts* that they should be boys. That is how they are in terms of their gender orientation and behaviour. This then becomes the basis of their identity. In the same way I have ministered to men who believed that they should be girls and have various predictable distortions of their personality.

Note:
There are other reasons for gender disorientation and preference.

A final note in relation to prenatal ministry if it presents as the source

Spiritually, God intended for us to be accepted, valued, received and loved right from our very beginnings. A rejective spirit is from another kingdom which is not the kingdom of God. In the event that our commencement to life and relationships was under rejection there is often a spirit there which also needs to be dealt with. Once the person is connected to the feelings and beliefs, postured to receive from God in whatever way He chooses to touch them, simply tell the spirit of rejection, fear or whatever else to go. Most times this is not a dramatic deliverance. For example, the person may suddenly have some emotion as the spirit leaves, cough as it comes out on the breath or exhibit involuntary deepened breathing. Quite often you will not see much happen but the person will simply report feeling lighter.

Am I 'qualified' to minister healing or freedom?

You do not need to have some big ministry to do this, as it is firstly, the work of the Holy Spirit, the finger of God. It is in the name of

Jesus Christ, not your name that you are commanding it to go. Remember redemption! Regardless of how you see yourself at the moment, the Father sees you as perfect, (Hebrews 10:14), seated in the heavenlies with Christ (Ephesians 2:6). Positionally, over all of the works of the enemy, in Christ, with authority over all of the power of the enemy (Luke 10:19). This is regardless of whether or not you are a brand-new Christian or having a good or bad day!

He made us and anointed us with the Holy Spirit so that we could do these good things! We just need the heart of God in wanting to see people helped by receiving His provisions. It is not about personal perfection or being good enough in our own eyes. This ability to have the Holy Spirit work through you, as you are, is the grace of God. He surely smiles and is pleased when we have enough faith to trust Him at His word.

Ephesians 2: 8-10, " *8 God saved you by his special favor when you believed. And you can't take credit for this; it is a gift from God. 9Salvation is not a reward for the good things we have done, so none of us can boast about it. 10 For we are God's masterpiece. He has created us anew in Christ Jesus, **so that we can do the good things he planned for us long ago**"* (NLT, Emphasis mine).

Peter had to realize his own human weaknesses, and all of God's supply and provision, before he was suitable to humbly serve God. Peter denied Jesus proving his humanity. In spite of this failure, Jesus' next instructions to him were to go and feed His sheep. Now aware that he was to work in the grace of God's provisions, the power of the Holy Spirit and the name of Jesus, he was ready to serve. He now was able to make the following statements which we should all humbly identify with:

Acts 3:12 *"So when Peter saw it, he responded to the people: "Men of Israel, why do you marvel at this? Or why look so intently at us, as though by **our own power or godliness** we had made this man walk"?*

Acts 3:16 *"And His name, **through faith in His name**, has made this man strong, whom you see and know. Yes, **the faith which comes through Him** has given him this perfect soundness in the presence of you all"* (NKJV, Emphasis mine).

Later we see this principle of total reliance on God and His righteousness was acknowledged by the Apostle Paul. Along with Peter, a key to his success was the knowledge of his own imperfect human nature. As with us, he was still undergoing the process of sanctification.

Acts 14:3, "*Therefore they stayed there a long time, speaking boldly in the Lord, who was bearing witness to the word of His grace, granting signs and wonders to be done by their hands.*"

Acts 14:15b, "*We also are men with **the same nature as you***" (NKJV, Emphasis mine).

They acknowledged willingly, that they had the same nature as these men. In the Greek language, the word translated nature means similarly *affected, like passions*. They were pointing out that they were aware of their human weaknesses and propensities, and without the Grace of God and the works of the Holy Spirit, these things would not be happening.

The point that I am making is that you don't step back from taking authority over an evil spirit because you are not perfect in your own eyes. That is the best place to be! His grace is sufficient for you. You are, through Jesus, perfect in God's eyes and that is all that matters. In the unlikely event that you are actually perfect in all of your ways, then you no longer need Jesus to make grace available to you. However, if that is the case, you most likely are in deception and have some serious pride issues which, incidentally, seem to be on the top of the list of things that God does not like!

A key to all kinds of ministry is to base your worthiness and consequent authority to minister, in the name of Jesus, on the completed work of redemption, as opposed to where you are up to in the ongoing work of sanctification. It is also wise to base your own worthiness in qualifying for any kind of healing or freedom, on the redemptive work of Jesus rather than where you have come to in your own version of being good enough. God very pointedly marks out that our own efforts at righteousness, as opposed to His provision through Jesus falls along way short.

Isaiah 64:6, **"All** *of us have become like one who is unclean, and all our righteous acts are like filthy rags; we all shrivel up like a leaf, and like the wind our sins sweep us away"* (NIV, Emphasis mine).

Romans 3:10 As it is written: *"There is* **no one righteous**, *not even one"* (NIV, Emphasis mine).

God Himself not only heals our diseases, He deals with the reason for the disease to begin with. I have never seen God not heal or free a person physically, emotionally or spiritually if they receive from Him with a simple faith. This includes people with some fairly unsanctified behaviour and attitudes at times.

Psalm 103:2-4, " ² *Praise the LORD, O my soul, and forget not all his benefits,* ³ *who forgives* **all** *your sins and heals* **all** *your diseases,* ⁴ *who* **redeems your life** *from the pit and crowns you with love and compassion* (NIV, Emphasis mine).

Addressing the evil spirit
Most times, if you have the person connected to their feelings and beliefs, and you address a spirit as we have said, you may see a sudden release of emotion, or they may simply report that they feel lighter or free. They may report that, at the moment that you told the spirit to go, God communicated with them in some way. It really doesn't matter whether you address the spirit in a whisper or a yell. It is not volume or some kind of show that releases the person, it is the place of authority that God has given that matters. Equally important is the permission of the person and their desire for you to address the spirit. It is largely a matter of exposing the spirit and its hold that makes the ministry effective.

I know, in different nations across the world, a number of little, very old ladies, who are very adept at casting out demons without changing the tone of their voices. So physical size, personality, emotional intensity or strength really are not relevant; it is really about understanding the authority that you have in the name of Jesus.

The example of the Canaanite woman, in Matthew chapter 15, is an excellent illustration of spiritual authority. The woman came with a presenting problem of a demon troubling her daughter. Jesus is not recorded as saying or praying anything regarding the demon or going to the lady's house. He simply said that as a response to the woman's faith that her child would be set free. There is no mention of a manifestation. Notably the story describes the result of the child being set free as healing. Other times we see demons come out just in the presence of Jesus or later the Apostles in the book of Acts.

Matthew 15:22, *"A Gentile woman who lived there came to him, pleading, "Have mercy on me, O Lord, Son of David! For my daughter has a demon in her, and it is severely tormenting her."*

Matthew 15:28, *"Woman," Jesus said to her, "your faith is great. Your request is granted." And her daughter was instantly healed"* (NLT, Emphasis mine).

Demonic amplification
Demonic dynamics will be discussed in more detail in later chapters. I want to point out that, the belief that matches the emotional breach is often the entry point for a demon stronghold. Dealing with the beliefs that give ground to the spirit is far more important than the spirit itself.

If you put your favourite songs through an amplifier, it is the same music, but now it has power. Evil spirits or demons, as we also know them, work in much the same way. You can have an emotional problem without having a spirit attached, which is going to be the case in most *Truth Encounters* sessions. You can hold the same belief, but the pain or response is now magnified by a demonic entity. This is why I believe people will often report some measure of emotional release or freedom in a prayer line, at a healing meeting or church service. The presence of the Holy Spirit has caused the evil spirit to move off.

Prior to our working in *Truth Encounters* we would cast out demons. Some people would report a measure of improvement, and others would be back in the same condition a week later. The problem was that we drove the rats away but didn't clean up the rubbish, being the negative beliefs causing the brokenness, pain or anxiety.

– Chapter 14: Sources of & Influences on Heart beliefs –

I am often in churches where the ministers proclaim that God is going to move and heal everyone's hurts and issues in the service. I have not yet seen this happen, although God can do absolutely anything so it is possible. The only predictable way that I have ever seen God completely freeing people from heart-based beliefs is through some kind of *Truth Encounter*.

Healed of Anorexia Nervosa
A number of years ago I was attending a healing meeting and I saw a man there with his wife and daughter whom I had seen in other healing meetings in another state. He also recognized me so we were chatting together. As we went along, he reported that he was there because his daughter had anorexia nervosa and had been hospitalized in a critical condition, as I recall more than once. I could see the desperation in his eyes and encouraged him to have faith and expect a breakthrough. I realized that he had brought her to a number of healing meetings with no result in the past.

My experience told me that people may get some partial help through deliverance in a prayer line, but that usually they are freed by dealing with the beliefs. Feeling that I should offer some help, I hesitantly said something along the lines of: *This is an excellent ministry, so there is every chance for her healing this weekend! But, if you don't get the breakthroughs that you are looking for, we see God bringing healing to these kinds of complaints in other ways.* And I gave him my card.

A month or two later I received an email reporting that she had been in hospital again and could we help. When we were near their town we dropped in and did a session with their daughter at their local church. We then headed off to minister somewhere else and heard nothing further. A year or so later we were in a meeting in their state and after the service the glowing mother came up to me and reported that from the time of her session, the daughter had simply improved and put on weight returning to health.

God can do anything, but personally I have not seen complete emotional healing in a normal prayer line. We do at times minister a *Truth encounter* in prayer lines but only on rare occasions, or if it has just been taught and people are aware of the source of their issues.

Important Note:
I never think about evil spirits when I am ministering in a *Truth Encounter*. I am focused purely on finding the beliefs. If there is one present, and you understand demonic dynamics, you will become aware that it is involved. Don't go looking for spirits. Most times with *Truth Encounters*, if there is a spirit implicated it will leave when the beliefs are resolved and you may not even be aware that there was one actively working [2]. This is because the spirit is usually involved in the sinful responses or reactions to the hurtful belief. Once the hurt is resolved they no longer need or want to respond in this way. So, you can see that the spirit has a hold because of their wilful cooperation. In a very practical way, the truth has made them free.

Examples of this could be issues such as; bitterness, unforgiveness, rebellion, pride, self-pity, anger, control, fear and so on. Most of the time these issues are present without any obvious demonic stronghold or amplification. Both you and the person being ministered to may never even become aware of the demonic presence that was possibly involved at some level. For more information on spiritual issues see section 3 on dealing with demonic influences.

---

[2] The depth of the pain can also have a bearing on the strength of a spirit and its power and influence in the host person.

CHAPTER 15
Memory

Most of the time we are helping people, and indeed the majority of their problems, are going to be found in beliefs learnt or interpreted as conclusions about their identity or the situation found in their memories. We will therefore examine how these beliefs may be deposited in the heart.

Some people question whether or not accessing memory in a ministry setting is a valid activity. If I asked most people what John 3:16 says, they would quickly respond; 'God so loved the World....' How do they know this? They remember it. How to find your way home, sit on a chair, speak, or do anything at all, is based on learning and remembering. Memory is therefore related to every single action that we perform, including breathing.

Some people put up questions such as why do we have to look back? They quote the Apostle Paul, who urges us to forget the things which are behind. In the following passage and its preceding verses, you will see that he is not talking about ignoring life-shaping memories. He is in fact talking about forgetting his achievements as a Pharisee which he now counts as *rubbish*.

Philippians 3:13-14, "*[13] Brethren, I do not count myself to have apprehended; but one thing I do, forgetting those things which are behind and reaching forward to those things which are ahead. [14] I press toward the goal for the prize of the upward call of God in Christ Jesus*" (NKJV).

Others comment that you shouldn't spend your whole life looking into the past. I agree that we should be moving on and working for the Gospel. But we also set aside specific times where we deliberately deal with issues from our past. I recently heard a comparison between a rowing boat and a canoe or Kayak race. In a rowing boat you are moving forward but looking back all the time. Whereas, in a canoe or Kayak you are looking at where you are going and moving forward. On occasions, however, even in a Kayak it is good to look back and see if anything from behind needs to be considered and dealt with. Checking what is going on behind out of sight that might affect the outcome of your race?

In terms of negative beliefs and emotions, it is a critical part of the healing process. The initial memory where a belief is taken in, is the place with the most detail for accurately examining and identifying the conclusion and consequent belief from the circumstances taken to heart.

It is good to note that memory does not simply relate to the past, it also has implications for the future. For example, if someone has had an event where they were perhaps publicly embarrassed, they will now be on the lookout for potential places or situations where this could happen again. This will then be a source of low-grade anxiety and will often be present in gatherings. The long-term effects of this will have an outworking in the physical body as being the end of the line for the sub-surface thought.

The scientists tell us that a small almond shaped section of nervous tissue in the brain named the *Amygdala* is responsible for memory and emotions. It is considered by some to be the fear centre. When something significant such as embarrassment occurs, the Amygdala is activated, and its response could be something such as; *That wasn't good; I better make a good memory of that so that I can make sure that it doesn't happen again!* From the initial event, memory projects the new belief about possible repeat situations out into the future to try to prevent a repeat occurrence.

All fears or responses to particular stressors have their beginnings in memory of some kind. The possible exception to this may be a fear that has passed through the generation line.

Critical events
The first time that we do anything is a significant moment in terms of encoding information about how we perceive that activity. Our early impressions of how we perform in areas such as the school environment for example, are a common place of memory where people arrive in a session. How our parents and teachers regarded and assessed our efforts will affect the way in which we view our person and ability to perform and meet requirements. We could perhaps be compared to a sibling who is academically interested

and gifted and come away with some kind of inferiority belief or low self-image. Typically, these would be unconscious inner thoughts such as; *I am not as good as others. I'm dumb, a loser, useless, not like other people, a failure,* etc. etc.

This certainly has impact when we are deciding about our identity as a child, and while our brain is plastic and impressionable. Later in life we will use those beliefs to interpret other critical first-time events such as sexuality. Usually if the initial experience is not positive, they will see those activities through the filter of their existing self-image beliefs, having already learnt that they are *inferior or cannot perform as others can*. They will use these pre-existing beliefs to reach a conclusion about whether or not the activity is positive and reinforcing or yet another place for anxiety.

Note:
In much the same way as parents and teachers should remove pressure and help a child see their academic endeavours in a positive light, the church should help their newly-weds with realistic expectations to help them to qualify their performance in the learning process of areas such as sexuality and relationships. This would hold true for other significant first-time events such as speaking or sharing in a Church service.

Traumas and Episodes
A number of years ago we were conducting our healing school and a Chinese lady came into the session with her husband. All the way through the teaching she would cough every few seconds, not being deliberately disruptive, just unable to prevent it. The next day she made an appointment to be on the ministry list to receive some help. As we interviewed her it came to light that she had been in an accident crushing her chest, and this was the beginning point for her coughing. She was a very brave lady and connected with the fear belief proceeding from the trauma, which was as I recall; *I am going to die.*

As she remembered the event and connected with the belief and feeling, we invited the Lord to bring His truth. In this instance, because she was connected with the event, a spirit of fear of death was exposed and manifested, and then came out. At the same time God communicated to her regarding the trauma belief. She was free and sat quietly throughout the day, finally testifying to her healing in the evening service. She was healed and freed from some other problems, and as a result, was so pleased that she translated all of the considerable amount of school notes into Chinese for use in her own nation.

Notes:
1. It is unlikely that if we had gone after the spirit of fear that we would have had the same success in seeing her set free from it. Identifying and feeling the belief which the spirit rode in on at the point of weakness exposed it, and brought it into the open with nowhere to hide. Dealing with the belief closed the emotional breach that gave it place.

2. We are not hunting for demons, even in traumatic situations, we are looking for the beliefs encoded as that is where the problem really lies. If there is some evidence of demonic replay, stronghold or amplification then simply tell it to go. I usually do this while I have the person focus on the beliefs producing the feelings. This way the spirit is exposed. The same can be applied to dealing with areas such as lust problems. Being exposed to pornography for example can be a type of trauma which is deeply encoded in the memories. If there is a lustful spirit there then having the person think the thoughts from the trauma can in some cases cause the demon to be brought to the surface because you have connected with that which it holds!

3. Let me reiterate here, don't go looking for demons, but be aware that they may be present particularly in regards to trauma. Most *Truth Encounters* you will not even give demons a thought. (More on Spiritual dynamics in Section three).

Episodes

By *episodes*, I am referring to individual events where beliefs were the conclusions arrived at in that critical moment. For example, sexual or physical abuse which are usually extremely traumatic in nature. Your parents, forgetting to pick you up for school, might be a one-time episode where you conclude that you're *not important, and really don't matter*. But it may not be traumatic, because even though you are feeling hurt because of the omission, you are having a great time with the other kids in the playground.

Sexual abuse

To be abused sexually is a traumatic episode which can affect many areas of the personality. From the damage and brokenness involved, there emanates rejection, fear, confusion, degradation and low self-image. This is a significant area, when you consider that indications in the western world are that, as many as minimally fifty percent of women have had some form of inappropriate sexual behaviour acted out on them. This could range from being touched by a friend of the family or relative right through to penetrative sex with a small child. Having ministered to a great many of these victims, I can offer hope that God will faithfully set you free. I also offer a list of possible beliefs that are commonly present with people who have been offended against in this way.

Inferiority
I am dirty, unclean, not like other people, ruined, a nothing, and I'm bad.

Confusion
I am overwhelmed, and don't know or understand what is happening.

Guilt
Somehow this is my fault. I have done this. At times children will get attention, value and importance, at a neighbours' house when they have been receiving none at home. This may include sexual behaviour. The guilt is too much to bear because they know that at some level that they wanted to be there. On occasions I have ministered to people who have felt guilty because they have felt physical pleasure in the act. Nerve endings are nerve endings; they do not discriminate between whether an event is appropriate or not, they simply report sensations. So, if they felt pleasure then it was not their fault either, but this is something that they need perspective from the Lord on. More often abused people would report pain.

Fear
This can be in the form of being overwhelmed physically and emotionally and not understanding what is happening. Beliefs such as; *I cannot cope, it is too much to bear, I am trapped, overpowered, there is nobody here to protect me,* may also be present. Further, fear from threats from the perpetrator over being harmed if they

tell anyone, or being afraid to tell parents because it is a relative or even that they expect punishment from their harsh family may also be present.

If the abuse continues, with subsequent events, usually these later times are interpreted through whatever beliefs are already held from the initial episode. This could be the person believing that it is happening again because; they are bad, dirty, naughty or some other belief that *they* already hold as being true about themselves.

Some of the sad outcomes from sexual abuse are that once a person has concluded at heart level that they are bad or dirty, then why even try to be good; after all they are ruined and spoilt anyway. The result of this kind of inner dialogue can be a promiscuous lifestyle. Perhaps they have learnt that sexual acts give you favour, *love* or acceptance from men.

The exact opposite of promiscuity is the issue that you most commonly deal with, and that is sexual dysfunction. The act of sex by association connects you with all of the fears, feelings of sex as being dirty, guilt and defilement. Enjoyment and participation of sex is no longer an option for you. This can be a great barrier to having a wholesome, complete and intimate relationship with your spouse. Sadly, in this age a high percentage of males have also been abused.

I ministered to a man some time ago who reported that before he and his wife were married, they had had a very active sex life. (I am not making comments on the appropriateness of this behaviour here). After they were married, she shut down and the sex life that they had enjoyed ended. Once I had ascertained that she had been abused as a child, I explained to him that most probably before they were married, she felt as though she was in control and could walk away at any time. After they were married, she would have unconsciously been feeling as though she didn't have a choice any more, wasn't in control, and now she had to have sex. Possibly she also felt that she was trapped and couldn't get away. These were all unconscious thoughts that she had learnt in the abusive episode. Unintentionally her inner beliefs were now being triggered and her emotional priorities dictated her behaviour. Whatever the inner thinking, God has a greater truth to set you free.

Repetitive themes
God Himself encouraged repetition as a means of making our beliefs permanent memory, or our *default position*. For example, we recall Joshua being told five times to be strong and courageous. In other words, meditate on your responses until they are an automatic neural pathway. God is saying here that you need to set up a *shortcut* to how to react when you are under attack. Then, you no longer need to think it through, it is already decided who you are and how you are and for that matter how God views you. Repetitive themes from childhood, when our brains are *plastic*, malleable, and particularly impressionable, become long term beliefs that we hold.

Deuteronomy 6: 6-9, "*[6] And these words which I command you today shall be in your heart.*" [7] "*You shall teach them diligently to your children, and shall talk of them when you sit in your house, when you walk by the way, when you lie down, and when you rise up.*" [8] "*You shall bind them as a sign on your hand, and they shall be as frontlets between your eyes.*" [9] "*You shall write them on the doorposts of your house and on your gates*" (NKJV, Emphasis mine).

God is instructing Israel to have repetitive exposure to His commands so that they become heart beliefs and permanent pathways. Someone once said to me; *isn't filling up with scripture like brainwashing!?* I am not sure about you but by the time I began walking seriously with the Lord my brains needed washing! In any case I would also like to highlight from the passage, the command to *diligently* teach them to the children. God the creator of our beings knew how important it is for our children to receive His word in that critical time of plasticity when we are deciding about life. Prevention, and being able to walk with God minimizing areas of serving the enemy, leaves us less open to being hurt, and in a much better place to be fruitful. However, even if we are incorrectly programmed God is always holding out His hand offering healing and help.

Repetition in Modern life
For many people the very important pre-adolescent time is a period where they are being told or shown that nothing that they are doing is good enough. We have educational systems which cater for people whose minds think along particular lines. Most likely, very similar to the academics and educators who prepared the system. History is littered with billionaires, inventors, entrepreneurs and successful people who did not function well at, or even complete, school.

For many people, school for example, is a place where they can be repeatedly confronted with learning that they are second rate or inferior. Families that have high demands on performance or perfection and don't offer love, encouragement and acceptance are environments of repetitive reinforcement of this inadequacy.
I remember my son when he was first learning to ride a bike. He wobbled around the front yard taking out the new tree that my wife had planted. He then disappeared down the sideway from where an enormous crash emanated. When I went around to find out if he was alright, he had ridden into the BBQ knocking it into the tin shed. He made some kind of statement such as; *I can't do it, I suck! My response to him was something along the lines of; you're doing great, it took me more goes than that to get as far as you did! Really?* he said looking encouraged. What just happened? I guarded his heart by helping him interpret the situation in a positive light.

Note:
Before you feel that you have failed on your own parenting journey, I was not always so impressive with my parenting skills; we all have to learn.

The point is that if we are always encouraging, always finding the positives, then we are keeping their heart self-beliefs in God's order. As the Apostle Paul put it:

2 Corinthians 10:8, "... *for even if I boast somewhat freely about the authority the Lord gave us for building you up rather than pulling you down, I will not be ashamed of it* ..." (NIV, Emphasis mine).

Many people have only ever experienced criticism and disapproval, being programmed over and over again with their shortcomings and failings. Those who are around my age or older grew up in *the little children should be seen and not heard* generation. The implication of this statement is that you are some kind of second-class citizen as a child, not significant, valuable or important. And that is exactly what a great many people believe inside, that they simply don't matter, or that they are a nuisance, in the way, unacceptable or feel as though they are *a nothing*. Those who were meant to be guarding their hearts were unwittingly programming them through repetitive reinforcement that in some way they are not good enough.

In defence of all parents I would like to add that most fathers and mothers love their children. They would not deliberately hurt their families and would certainly have done things differently if they understood the ramifications. In some measure the church is responsible for having failed to teach its members how to protect their children in this vital area. In any case, most are likely parenting out of that which they received themselves, and the modelling that has passed through the generation lines.

Today, most children receive their training from media, much of which is run by people from the *children should be seen and not heard* generation and is slanted towards *my rights* generation which is a knee jerk reaction to being made to feel second rate. It is not too surprising to see this response from children of that era, leading to giving children full rights and decision-making authority long before they have the knowledge and wisdom to cope with running their own lives.

Possibly, an inner decision to not put that inferiority onto their children came as a result. Consequently, many modern children grow up under the belief that they are special. They are special to God, but in life they are no more special than anyone else, and when they grow up it is often a shock for them to find this out. We, as the Church have to take responsibility for equipping our people in how to Biblically train our children and bring them up in the counsel of the Lord.

Upgrade information
We don't want to confuse the healing of our heart beliefs with the renewing of our minds. There are many things that we learn through life that are not deeply recorded. We are talking here about areas such as identity beliefs. This is for God to free us from. But if we simply have wrong beliefs about how to do life then receiving improved information will renew our minds.

Let me say here that most of the changes in how we live and see things come to us through reading our Bibles or hearing the word taught. If this were not so, then why would we even bother to preach and teach. All that we are talking about here relates to areas and issues that we cannot overcome through better information. If we read in the Bible that we should build each other up and not judge each other, we might think; *well that is a better way of living than that which I am doing now!* And having made the decision we become a hearer and doer of the Word.

There is a great old story of a lady who was cooking a roast. Her friend was watching her and asked her; *why do you cut the roast in half before you put it in the oven?* The lady replied; *I actually don't know, my mother always did it that way so I will have to ask her!* When the question was presented to the mother her response was; *Oh, I only have a small oven, so I have to cut it in half, but you have a big oven and that is not necessary for you!*

The lady just received better information on how to do life. To keep this ministry in balance and perspective, there is still a preeminent place for Biblical advice (Counselling) and Bible teaching. In fact, on many occasions as we go along with the healing ministry there is a concurrent thread of teaching running through the sessions. I have unfortunately known of people who become proficient in the *Truth Encounters* ministry who have, as a result, felt that they are qualified to give advice on, for example, relationships. Some of them do not have sound Biblical knowledge and consequently their own relationships are not in order. This is something that Pastors who allow groups to minister under the covering of their church may need to take note of. Beware that a person who is equipped and now helping and seeing people set free is not going beyond the guidelines that you allow for the ministry.

CHAPTER 16
Types of Beliefs

Other ministries use different names for identifying types of beliefs. Over 20 years of working in this area we have found that they commonly fall into one of the following categories. It helps to know what type of belief you are dealing with because you then understand the kind of circumstances in a memory that you are looking for.

Identity beliefs – about self

Identity beliefs relate to that which you perceive about who you are and how you are. Rather than a lengthy discourse let me suggest some common beliefs reflecting how one's identity is seen:

"I'm not loveable, I'm unacceptable, not enough, less than others, stupid, a nothing, dumb, ugly, a failure, a loser, useless, weak, I don't matter, am not important" and so on. Notice that they are all beliefs relating to your identity, about 'self.'

These types of *heart* beliefs are at the root of many anxieties. Unconsciously you are worried about people discovering your shortcomings or reinforcing them. When I am preparing people for ministry, I often explain identity beliefs to people using a story which I have constructed but is based on stories that I have heard over and over again.

Sample story

Imagine someone who has come to you is reporting how much anxiety they are going through. How I would deal with it may run something like this;

Fred: I have a terrible problem with anxiety.
Me: Can you give me an example of how it affects you?
Fred: I was at work the other day and heard the main door behind me open; I had an anxiety attack and reached for my pills.
Me: If you stop and think about the situation for a moment, what was it that you were worried about when you heard the door open?"

Fred:	Thoughtful pause; Mmmmmm...I was nervous that it may have been the boss.
Me:	And if it was, what are you worried about happening?
Fred:	He may have come over and looked at my work!
Me:	And if he did, what do you think could happen?
Fred:	He might tell me that it was no good.
Me:	I am sure that that is not a good feeling. I want you to close your eyes and feel what it is like for him to tell you that your work is not good enough and let your mind connect you with other historical places where you have felt just like that.
Fred:	Pause; I have just remembered that when I was in kindergarten, I was doing a painting with some other kids and the teacher was coming along looking at everyone's work. The first person was Mary and the teacher said that Mary's painting was so creative, and then Johnnie's was so neat and all in the lines. When she saw mine, she said, it was the biggest unrecognizable mess that she had ever seen in her life!
Me:	As you look at that criticism and rejection, I want you to look for the conclusion and belief about yourself that you came to.
Fred:	With some emotion; I'm useless, not as good as others.
Me:	Let's ask the Lord what He considers to be true about you being useless and inferior. Just concentrate on those beliefs and feelings and listen.
Fred:	Pause; He said, why would He have called and chosen me if I was useless. He said that all of His children are created equal, they have different gifts but none are better than another. I have just remembered that I was the best reader in the group!
Me:	So how do you feel about people discovering that you are useless and not as good as them now?
Fred:	Honestly, I feel that I am fine just as I am. And I am just the same as everyone else, the same only different, different in a good way, unique!

Identity beliefs also have a bearing on our relationships and how we respond, react to, and deal with others. They also reflect on how we relate to ourselves, and ultimately God. Truly, *as a man thinks in his heart, so is he*, in terms of how he reacts to others, and also how he sees himself.

Proverbs 23:7, "*For as he thinks in his heart, so is he*" (NKJV).

Let us propose that a person thinks that they are not good enough because they do not do things well enough. By now we know that this is a belief that was learnt in an event earlier in life. As a result, if that person feels, whether it is true or just a perception, that you are criticizing something that they are doing then you can expect some kind of angry response. They are angry at you for making them feel that which they already unconsciously believe, but they are also angry at themselves for not being able to do things well enough. Whenever negative emotions are present, they may be directed outwardly as a reaction, but they also exist inwardly connected to an area of hurt as well. So, this person might struggle to forgive you for how you are making them feel, but they probably haven't any forgiveness for themselves either for being the person who you can find fault with, because of their perceived imperfections and shortcomings.

This will also reflect in your relationship to God. You will be a double minded man. In your human spirit, which is now one with the Holy Spirit, you know that you are loved and accepted. But in your heart, you believe that you are not good enough because you cannot do things well enough. Therefore, how could God consider you as good enough, when you don't believe that you are yourself at heart level!

James 1:6, *"But let him ask in faith, with no doubting, for he who doubts is like a wave of the sea driven and tossed by the wind. 7 For let not that man suppose that he will receive anything from the Lord; 8 he is a double-minded man, unstable in all his ways"* (NKJV).

Sometimes we believe in God's goodness mentally, but the lack of faith in our hearts is because of our doubts about our worthiness to receive. Jesus pointed out that we can have whatever we believe in our hearts, not our heads. So, for faith to flow we have to believe that God is greater than our hearts. We need to receive His truth about our value and worth.

Mark 11:22-23, *"22 So Jesus answered and said to them, "Have faith in God." 23 "For assuredly, I say to you, whoever says to this mountain, 'Be removed and be cast into the sea,' and does not doubt in his heart, but believes that those things he says will be done, he will have whatever he says"* (NKJV, Emphasis mine).

We had not been involved in this ministry all that long, when one day I noticed my wife getting a bit agitated as I was wiping down the kitchen bench. I commented to her that I could see that me doing this was making her angry. After a short time, we identified that to her it seemed as if I was implying that she was not doing a good enough job, that she was an untidy person. After a short period of ministry into the memory where she had first learned this, and truth from the Lord, her whole attitude changed. Now instead of being upset, she felt it could be a good idea while I was helping to sweep the floor and put out the rubbish as well.

Situational beliefs

As the name suggests, these are beliefs which have come out of a situation and may or may not relate to your identity. Phobic beliefs fall under this category. An example of this type of belief might be something such as having panic attacks in small spaces where you feel captive, such as an elevator. As you focus on the feeling you might, for example, identify that the anxiety about small spaces might be that you will not be able to breath. As your mind does a data match with other places holding those feelings you remember as a small boy playing football at school. You managed to get hold of the ball and five or six boys jumped on you and held you down. In that moment you were crushed, trapped and struggled to breathe. As you focus on the situation, we ask you what will happen if you can't get away and breathe. The response is; "I can't breathe, I am going to die!"

There is nothing here relating to identity, it is all to do with the situation. As we have the person embrace the fear feeling and the belief that they are trapped, can't get away, and are going to die because they cannot breathe, we ask God for His truth. Which could simply be words, or a realization that they did not die, or some other communication that sets them free?

Story

Some time ago I was waiting with our lady bank manager in her office for some other staff to come in to work out a financial proposition that we were putting together for a church development. While we were waiting, we were casually chatting and she made the comment; *I see that you travel overseas quite a lot.* I affirmed her statement, and she went on to say that she would love to be able to travel but she has a fear of flying. I said to her that our ministry experience is that often when people are afraid to fly that it usually began with a traumatic memory along the lines of perhaps a child being in a swimming pool and getting out over their heads. They can no longer touch the sides and they cannot swim. They feel like they are out of control and are going to die. When they go on an airplane their mind automatically makes the connection. *You are not in control, can't touch the bottom, there is nothing solid beneath you and therefore you could die!*

She looked at me in amazement and said; *I just remembered when I was a small girl, I lived in the country and was in the local swimming pool. I went out too far into the deep end and thought that I was going to die!*

The point is, it is a belief from a situation, nothing to do with identity. These are just simple terms we use to differentiate between types of beliefs. Incidentally, there can be many other situations that can produce a fear of flying. I recently encountered a lady with three different reasons from three individual memories that caused her to be afraid of flying.

A few years ago, my wife ministered to a lady who had a fear of flying. Her husband was very frustrated because they were getting older and he was eager to go adventuring. She received ministry for this fear and some other issues and then they went home. We did not see them again for a number of years, but eventually we ran across them again. I remembered her fear of flying and enquired about how she was going with it. She responded excitedly that they had now been around the world several times.

Objection beliefs
These are beliefs where for some reason there is an objection held that stops the person from proceeding to the memory or receiving from the Lord. An example of this could be something as simple as somebody believing that they are doing the wrong thing if they allow the possibility that their parents were anything less than perfect. Before they will go to places where, perhaps their identity was damaged, you will need to find out and deal with why they think that being real about their parents is doing the wrong thing. You are not seeking to dishonour them, rather find the source of your own problems.

At other times people will come into a session and you can observe that they are very tense. Sometimes I will simply suggest something along the lines of; *do you believe that you won't be able to do this ministry?* or *Are you afraid that I will be disappointed if you cannot do this?* They often look a bit surprised but respond with a ready; *Yes! How did you know?*

We need to deal with the fear of failure memory first. This may be a place where they may have disappointed someone by not being able to do what was expected, or perhaps a place where everyone else could achieve and they could not, or something similar.

I recall one man being hesitant to let himself connect with his memory. I asked him what he believed that made him object to seeing the content of his historical event. He reported that he was afraid. I requested that he focus on the fear and identify and clarify exactly what it was that produced the anxiety. He told me that he was afraid that he would be out of control, which was clearly to do with what was going on in the memory. I asked him to focus on the belief and invited the Lord to bring His perspective. The man sat quietly for a moment and then opened his eyes and looked up at the same time making the statement; *I **am** out of control!*

This communication from the Lord meant something to the man in his inner parts. It was good truth as we all have very limited control over the World we live in, even the actions of those close to us. We never really know if an aircraft is about to come through our roof or the stock market may have just crashed and we have missed the news! The truth is that we are all largely not in control, but God is, and He is able to protect us. This resolved the resistance issue and the man proceeded into his memory for freedom.

Perhaps a final story in order to illustrate another way that *objection beliefs* may present and impact the ministry time. First, I note that you do not need to look for these; you will simply observe that they are present. And secondly, you will not run across them in every session, they will be involved occasionally.

Objections to letting God speak to you
Periodically you will encounter people who hold beliefs that prevent them from receiving from God. These could be simple thoughts such as; *I'm not worth His time, of course He will free others, but He*

doesn't care about me, and everyone else can do it, (hear from God) but I won't be able to!

These beliefs have been learnt in specific memories that are best dealt with first. You may recognize that there is some kind of blockage to them hearing from God, and this is probably the main cause. Still other people hold beliefs that God does not interact with people today, or at times we run across those who have been trained in another ministry model and refuse to listen for God's voice because; *this is not the way we do it!*

Story

A number of years ago, we were ministering to an attractive young lady who was needlessly jealous of other women. She was successfully ministered to and received freedom in other areas but her jealousy problem remained. It caused major problems in her relationship with her fiancée who could not even watch the news on television because there might be a pretty weather girl. If there was a magazine around with a girl on the cover it was quickly put away. If they were at church, he was watched constantly in case he looked at another girl. If she even thought that he may have noticed another girl, real or imagined she flew into a rage. As a perceived solution to her jealousy she had become very controlling in her relationship.

We identified the source as being a time where, as a small girl of around 3 or 4 years old, the family would receive visits from a friend who was a handsome young man. He would fool around playfully with the little girl and gave her attention which made her feel special and loved. She concluded that this special affection and attention was only for her. One day the young man brought his girlfriend along with him. The family had known that he had a girlfriend but the little girl did not. For her, this was an intensely traumatic moment. She was devastated that someone else clearly had a greater measure of the attention and affection of the young man. She was overcome with jealousy. We could summarize jealousy as; *you have what I would like to have.* She also felt incredibly inferior. Here was a mature adult girl with modern clothes and a fully-grown shapely figure. She concluded along the lines that, she was; *Not enough, and could not be what she needed to be. The other girls were better.*

Later, as an attractive adult woman herself, this thinking was unreasonable. She continued to fear losing her male partner and to be jealous of other girls who could take him away because, unconsciously in her heart, she was afraid that he would see another girl who was more, and prefer her. This for her was a logical inner conclusion which matched her historical event. Having identified and confirmed these beliefs with her we invited God to communicate the truth to her to set her free.

In other things that we had dealt with her she had no problem in hearing from God and receiving her healing, but this was different. So up to this point we can see that she didn't have an issue with going to the original memory or accepting her beliefs. Now, however, she held an *objection* to having God speak to her and receive freedom from her jealousy and resultant ungodly control.

We eventually worked out that she believed that if she let go of the control through healing, then her fiancée would go ahead and prefer another girl. So, for her, the jealousy was tied in with what she perceived to be true, and control over the situation that she was insecure about, was her solution to the problem. She simply did not want to be free because she felt that staying in control was going to protect her from losing her man. Sometime later when she realized that she would lose her man anyway because of her jealousy and control, she committed her will to the process. She then received truth about her beliefs and was delivered of the spirit holding the jealousy and controlling behaviour.

I want to point out that the spirit was not the problem, her will was the issue. The spirit had come in on the sins of jealousy and control, beginning with the emotional breach that was created with the shock of discovering the adult girlfriend. She was deceived unwittingly into believing that controlling her male boyfriends was the solution to the perceived situation. This opened her to cooperating and participating with a sinful attitude inspired by an unholy spirit.

As long as she believed that the control served a purpose for her, the spirit had ground to magnify, amplify and hold her bound. As the spirit worked through her it also held the fiancée in bondage, not being free to relate with females in a normal way or even watch television. Simply trying to cast out the spirit without identifying the belief that gave it place is normally a fruitless exercise. In a sense she held the spirit to herself believing that it was serving a purpose for her. Of course, she was unaware of the spiritual element of what was happening. Once she permitted herself to be freed of the beliefs behind the jealousy there was no need for the *protection* afforded by the controlling attitudes.

The same is true with deliverance from all sin-based issues. Until you are wilfully convinced that you need to fall out of agreement with the sin, then you will most probably stay in bondage. It is vitally important therefore, to understand that genuine repentance is the basis of deliverance. Repentance in the Greek language means; *change your thinking, reconsider your ways.* Often, we are unwilling or unable to do that until we discover what it actually is that we are thinking in the heart that puts us in a place of harbouring or hosting ungodly actions that give place to the devil. Hence, this is one application of the verse; *you shall know the truth and the truth shall make you free.*

2 Timothy 2:25, *"In meekness instructing those **that oppose themselves**; if God perhaps will **give them repentance** to the acknowledging of the truth, 26 And that they may recover themselves out of the snare of the devil, who are taken captive by him at his will"* (KJV, Emphasis mine).

Note:
The word of God teaches us what sin is so that we will know what manner or type of spirit we are cooperating with.

Luke 9:55, *"But He turned and rebuked them, and said, "You do not know what manner of spirit you are of"* (NKJV).

Note:
Not all controlling behaviour or jealousy has a spirit resident inside the person. It is still cooperating with an unholy spiritual influence even if it is weaker and from outside the host person.

However, if as in this case there is a blockage, or there is an unusually strong resistance to ministry, you may find that a spirit on the inside is the cause. It is more attached to the responses or solutions to the hurt rather than the pain itself. Chasing the spirit will not bring the freedom; dealing with the hurt that produces the need for the ungodly reactions and activities, which sometimes opens the door to an evil spirit, is the most important focus. Once the truth is received, freeing the person from the troubling belief, then the spirit may manifest, or simply leave once the reason for its presence, is removed.

Going to the deep place where the belief resides

This ministry can be carried out anywhere and at any time. For the best possible results, I find that a quiet room, in preferably a one on one situation affords the person receiving ministry the best possible opportunity to concentrate without distraction. I do remember situations such as ministering to a man who was suicidal on the side of a very busy street. There were noisy cars and motorbikes' roaring past, but the man seemed to be unaffected, and to my amazement, was able to focus on the source of his pain and receive his freedom.

Normally we try to have a quiet room. Having heard their story and made a few notes about areas that may need ministry I encourage them to go to what I call, *periscope depth*. In other words, close their eyes, shut out the outer world and concentrate on the inner deeper place of the heart.

Beliefs, feelings and memories

At times, as you hear the story and the presenting problems, you will note statements that reflect inner beliefs. At other times, some emotion will come up, but it does not seem to be at that time connected to the belief. I liken this to those multi story concrete car parks that are in many cities today. Each level has a number which is usually painted on the various doors to the stairs and exits on that level. It is almost as if, from this door over here, you hear a belief statement that does not hold feelings. But from another door over there proceeds some emotion. They do not seem to be connected here on level 5, but as you ask questions and embrace the thoughts and feelings eventually you end up in the basement, at the initial memory where the first-time belief was taken to heart. So, the basement holds the circumstances in the memory which produced the conclusion, which became a permanent belief that produces and matches the emotions.

Secondary memories holding the same beliefs

Often people will not go directly to the first memory where the belief was interpreted and encoded. For example, someone who believes that they are not as good as other people may have memories later in life or even recently that seemed to confirm this thinking. This could be a marriage break up or failure to perform in secondary school. You could be stopping off here to connect more intensely with the emotions or to refine the belief. Ultimately, as we have previously stated, their identity beliefs will have begun before the age of 10 years old.

For many years, we fostered both long term and short-term children, so we can confirm from experience that what both the Bible and science say about this being the critical formative age is true. Into your family come children who are *pre-packaged* with their inner thinking about themselves and life. The same can be said about everyone who walks through the door of your church. *Something happened* that they most likely didn't ask for; they are clothed by life. Our mission is to be equipped to help them, offering God's answers and provision.

Very commonly, the beginning point for a ministry session is the report of the subject, having been triggered in a relationship or particular situation. In the event that the emotion from the belief is strong in the current relationship, but not so strong in the initial memory, you can have the person switch backwards and forwards from the strong feelings from the present time to the event held in memory state. This will help to identify and accept the accuracy of the thoughts and feelings from the source.

Interpreting other people's lives through our own beliefs

We have already highlighted that our lives, behaviour and responses are shaped by what we believe in our heart. It also affects how we perceive the situations of other people, and indeed how we see life.

Proverbs 4:23, *"Above all else, guard your heart, for it affects everything you do"* (NLT, Emphasis mine).

A person who grew up in poverty will be able to empathize with poorer people in the World. A Pastor who grew up being treated as though he was not important or significant, will not let anyone out of the door on Sunday, until they have been greeted and made to feel that they are valuable.

What we believe about ourselves and life is projected onto others even if they do not hold the same beliefs. We expect that they would feel the same as us. Someone who grew up with injustice will consider it vital to stand up for those who are oppressed.

On a number of occasions, I have had mothers come to me in a very distraught condition because their daughters are going through a marriage break up. When I suggest that these situations are probably stirring up beliefs within them, I usually receive a response along the lines of; *shouldn't a mother be feeling this for their child?* Yes, they should, but I encourage them to take the opportunity to investigate and see if any of the feelings that are present are connected to their own experiences. Usually once we have worked through all of the emotions that the situation has provoked in them, they are only left with a mental sympathy for their child's circumstances. In other words, *all* the feelings that they were experiencing were tied to interpreting what their daughters should be going through by their own inner beliefs. The daughters probably have their own historically based reactions to the situation.

Common beliefs, different personalities
After a period of time doing this ministry, you begin to find repetitively that there are some very common beliefs that you deal with over and over again. What does change is the differing personalities of the people that you are working with. Some people are very emotional while others have little emotion and are largely cognitively mind-based people.

I have seen at times that some *brands* of inner healing seem to think that if you cry you are being touched by the Holy Spirit and being healed. In much the same manner people can think that a person crying in the church service is being healed by the Holy Spirit. That is possible, but I think that most times the presence of the Spirit may be softening emotions. We tend to bless the emotion and pray something such as; *more Lord, bless them more, heal them Lord.* If we asked them a few questions we may find that, for example, it was that song about the Father that moved them, because their father left when they were a child, or something similar.

The key to the healing is identifying the belief, not the degree of the emotion. Someone who experiences feelings intensely may struggle with emotions daily. A more stoic person may simply get on with life but have issues, such as anxiety, or belief-based behaviour such as the need to succeed, be regarded, or be right. The emotional person may have a dramatic time in the ministry session and express a great sense of relief and freedom.

The more cognitive person may only feel enough to identify and resolve the belief. They may not report much more than that the belief no longer feels true. Just because they lack the euphoria does not mean that they are not free. They are more likely to experience what has happened in terms of how they see life, their sense of peace and wellbeing, and notice that old responses and reactions have disappeared when certain stressors are present.

Ways in which we remember

1. Emotionally:
Fear, anxiety, rejection, grief, unworthiness etc. We access memory by connecting with the initial places that hold these feelings.

2. Pictures:
Memory events from very early life may just be a vague impression rather than a clear picture. Some people have incredibly vivid memories with amazing recall of detail. This can relate to the level of trauma and corresponding strength of the picture. Some people can have memory pictures that are not connected to emotions. They may have pushed the emotions down because they are too frightening or painful to look at.

One lady I was working with told me the story of having to get her own birthday cake as a child because her birthday had been forgotten. She was laughing about it as though it were a funny story. The emotions did not match the situation. She should have been feeling hurt and sad. It is necessary to accept the true feelings in the memory to identify that which you have believed.

3. The body:
(Somatic) headache, stress, breathing, tension, stress, muscles, nausea, aches and pains, etc. Have you ever had that sick, dread

feeling in the pit of your stomach? This is a probably body memory connecting you to a belief learnt in a previous situation. In a ministry setting you would have the person focus on this feeling and look for other places where they may have felt the same.

4. Senses:
Smells, sounds, taste, and touch etc. A commonly used example of this is music from your past which may make you feel happy or sad. The song is associated with a time in your life which may have been positive or negative. It may relate to bringing you to a visual event that contains something significant. Some people do not like to be touched or hugged. It connects them to times where touch may have meant something negative. You can have them focus on the thought of being touched and this will often bring a memory to them which contained these feelings.

5. Words:
Some phrases or unkind nicknames may be joined to unpleasant memories that are to do with the shaping of heart beliefs.

Sample questions
As you begin to work in this ministry, or even examine your own thoughts, you will find that there are only a certain number of questions available to use and I suggest some here. You can of course be creative and come up with your own.
"What will happen if ... ?" (e.g. ...'you have to fly overseas').

Note:
We call fear the **what if spirit!** so **what will happen if?** is a good basic question for fear, anxiety, stress or insecurity.

"How does it feel to think that ...?"	(e.g. ...'there is nobody to protect you').
"How does this make you feel ... ?"	(e.g. ...'to think that you don't matter').
"Why do you think ... ?"	(e.g. ...'no one cares about you').
"What does this mean about you ... ?"	(e.g. ...'that everyone else is able to succeed').
"What does it make you ... ?"	(e.g. ...'if you are the person who is ignored').

"What do you believe is true about you ... ? (e.g.... if someone has perhaps, learnt that they are stupid in an event).

Typical belief samples

Fear:	"This or that could happen!"
Anger:	"They don't care about me!" "This is not how things should be!"
Rejection:	"Nobody wants me, I don't belong, am not a part of this."
Stress:	"I can't cope!" "It's hopeless." (Depression)
Sadness:	"I am not loved."
Rebellion:	"It's not fair!"
Performance anxiety / inferiority:	"I cannot do what others can do."
Insecurity:	"People aren't doing what they should be doing."
Bitterness/resentment:	"I will not forgive them for what they have done" or at times, "what they have not done that they should have!"

All of these kinds of perceived beliefs affect relationships and often produce sin responses and reactions.

The demeanour of the minister

If you are going to be effective in this ministry you will need to become a good listener. Slow to speak and quick to listen is great wisdom. You hear what a person is saying to gather information and note cues that may point to beliefs. In addition, you are looking to God for prompts, inspiration and information. I have already discussed the car park analogy. Occasionally, once you gain some experience, it may be obvious to you what a person believes. However, if you suggest it, they may well deny it. It will not be until you arrive in the *basement* that the belief is alive and significant to them.

If you are not yet mature as a Christian, or indeed free from your own issues, you may have a need or tendency to be vocal about all that you know and think. This may not inspire the vital trust that is needed for a person to share their most intimate details. The need for confidentiality is absolutely critical. I have shared a number of testimonies and stories in this publication. If I think that a story might be helpful in the teaching and training environment, I will ask permission to share it. Without a person's consent I do not talk about details of anyone's ministry time. It is something personal between them and God. People coming for help will usually sense whether or not it is safe to open up the areas that their lives are built on with you.

Positioning

The most important area of any healing or freedom ministry is to have the person aligned to receive from the Lord. Jesus taught about the Kingdom of God before He ministered. It is vitally important that people understand what the issue is, and what God offers in terms of resolving your problem. Therefore, explaining or teaching about the ministry is key. This can come in the form of your own explanations, a work up book, video or audio teaching.

In an environment, such as attendees of our healing school, people who want ministry already know what to expect and how it works. In other settings, where possible, to be thorough and most effective, we will do a work up session first where we explain and teach about the ministry. We have found that God will not usually override a person's free will and choice. Consequently, He will only do for people that which they want and choose. This can be frustrating for some new ministers. They can see the answer to the problems and try to push people to deal with their issues. Jesus only ministered to those who came to Him. Given that He was preaching repentance, and many did not want to reconsider their ways or change their thinking about their lifestyles, many did not come. Our job is to teach what God has made available as best we can, and then be equipped to serve Him in helping those who come.

Being ready

Most people who have been through teaching on the subject or a workup session now see their problem and come to receive their freedom. Once in a while, I have someone who does the workup and, even though they now see the source of the issues, they feel that it is not something that they want to do. A small percentage never return, but many times they will return, weeks months or even years later, desperate, reporting that they are now ready to do whatever is necessary to be set free. I have come to realize that although we finish work for the day, the Holy Spirit goes home with them, and never ceases to work with and encourage them.

Common reasons why people may not come for ministry
1. Ignorance
They simply do not know about this opportunity for freedom or they have received a distorted picture of it from some source.

2. Alignment
It does not fit into their theological or ministry method framework.

3. Pride
Pride is the most common reason. Many people are full of their own opinions and views. Having some knowledge, they become *puffed up*. They want to fix the problem themselves without help from others, working it out in their own minds. Remember the Pharisees who considered themselves above the common sinners. Jesus at one time rebuked them for searching the scriptures because they thought that the written word alone would provide eternal life.

Pride says, *I will fix me!* in a sense, following on from the temptation in the garden to be *as or like God!* Pride wants to set up a monument to self to bow down to and be, in a way, your own god. Jesus pointed out that the scriptures actually do not fix you without Him, the word made flesh. He is the person whom the Holy Spirit can work through and meet your needs. The principle is the same for receiving the promise of eternal life, and also receiving other provisions that come through Jesus.

John 5:39-40, "[39] *You diligently study the Scriptures because you think that by them you possess eternal life. These are the Scriptures that testify about me,* [40] *yet you refuse to come to me to have life"* (NIV).

The beginnings or ground that gives place to pride is found in inferiority and low self-image. Pride, or making yourself above others, in your own thinking is the devil's solution for the perceived weakness that you hold about yourself at heart level.

Proud people are probably the ones who stay away from receiving help more than any others. Their behaviour, or how they appear, is often the exact opposite of a person's inner belief. For example, a person who walks around appearing self-important and superior almost certainly believes in their hearts that they are not important and are inferior. Now, the only viewpoint that holds any importance for them is their own. They will have the attitude that you better listen to them and often hold the floor in conversations. King Solomon was not kind in his appraisal of these hurting people in many of his writings.

Proverbs 26:12, *"Do you see a man wise in his own eyes? There is more hope for a fool than for him"* (NIV).

For a proud person to admit to any kind of weakness or imperfection strikes at the core of their sense of inferiority. And after all, what could anybody possibly know that they do not! The result is that many with pride issues avoid ministry. There can at times be an evil spirit involved in the resistance to help. Even if there is not a demon on the inside, pride certainly proceeds from spiritual influences even from the outside.

A while ago we had a new lady coming to our church who asked me if she could come for some help with her problems. She asked me if I could make sure that I don't tell the other leaders that she was coming. I replied with something like, *Sure, no problem. But I don't think that they would pay much attention, as many of the congregation comes for sessions and most of the leaders receive ministry themselves!* This seemed to put her at ease. The point is, isn't this what normal church life should look like anyway?

4. Control
We have already discussed that many people want to be in absolute control of their lives. For some of these persons, to be able to trust another, with the deep things of their lives is very difficult.

5. Fear
There are those who are simply too afraid of what might happen, what you might think about them, or what they may have to face to consider opening up for help.

6. Denial
Some people simply will not accept they have problems, or they may have a part in faulty relationships. These people expect that their

own emotional well-being would be fine if everyone around them did what they think they should be doing. This is called *projection*, where you deny your issues and blame shift your situation, feelings and responses onto everyone else. It is not surprising that we see the first instance of not taking responsibility for our own behaviour right back at mankind's beginnings in Genesis.

Genesis 3:11-12, *"[11] And he said, "Who told you that you were naked? Have you eaten from the tree that I commanded you not to eat from?"[12] The man said, "The woman you put here with me--she gave me some fruit from the tree, and I ate it"* (NIV).

Why do we need help?
Some people ask why they need to sit down with someone to do this ministry. Let me offer a couple of reasons.

1. If you don't commit to some kind of appointment then you will probably never get around to it. I used to say to people that it is a bit like going to the dentist, we put it off as long as we can. (Around 15 years ago I read of someone else making almost the exact same comparison).

2. To begin with, you most probably don't have the skills to find your beliefs, and you may find it hard to connect to deep painful events without experienced support. Eventually it may be possible to minister to yourself as it is a very simple process.

3. Discernment. If you've ever played the game of golf you will know that everyone will tell you how to improve and what you are doing wrong. Even bad golfers will give you advice, sometimes bad advice. The point is that they can see that you are doing something wrong. You cannot see your own swing, because you are in it. But they may not know what they are looking at.

Discernment in its simplest form, is being able to understand what you are seeing or looking at. It's a good idea to get your advice from a Golf pro whose own game is working well, rather than a *hacker* who is struggling with his handicap. Clearly the same is true in ministry; don't take advice from just any well-meaning Christian, it is worth checking the life and experience of the person that you are seeking help from.

Shopping lists

By the time a person has listened to teaching on *Truth Encounters* or has done a work up session, they should have a basic understanding of the ministry process. Many by now may have noteworthy memories coming to them. Anything that is a memory is significant or it would not be remembered to begin with. Few people can remember what they had for breakfast on a particular day 2 years ago; let alone many years ago because it really is not important.

We now ask the person to begin to put on their *shopping list* the areas that they may suffer with and are looking for freedom in. This can be known problems, such as never feeling that they are worth anything, or perhaps a fear of storms, or it can be a set of reactions that they have to specific situations.

A reaction example:

This may be something along the lines of; *I get very, very angry when my husband leaves his clothes on the floor.* This could come from some kind of belief such as, *nobody cares about me, and what I want.* A self-belief may be holding hurt behind that thinking, along the lines of; *I'm a nothing, I just don't matter.* The *I'm a nothing* is going to be the identity belief that holds the emotional pain. The anger is not the problem but is a predictable response to being made to feel like this.

Their *shopping list* may contain a list of issues that they are aware of, and also a number of trigger circumstances. We encourage them to simply write down any situations that produce negative emotions. Anything that makes them feel angry, sad, fearful, indignant, rejected, inferior, unimportant and so on. A *shopping list* could look something like;

I just never feel worthy of being noticed. (Looking for historical match).

My husband always seems uninterested in what I want....! etc. etc.

Some new ministers get nervous that they won't know what to do. As long as you remember that you are looking for the beliefs that produce the feelings, you are on the right track. We are not trying to give you methods, but rather principles. I am quite sure that my wife ministers very differently to me, but we are both looking for the same thing.

The people already have the problems so you don't have to find any. In addition, God has the answer for them already. Your job is only to help them find that which they believe in their hearts, then open it up to God to provide His truth. You can only minister to whatever they come in with for help. You may discern other issues, but if they do not want assistance in those areas, then you acknowledge their choices.

We can summarize the areas of responsibility along these lines;

Our part:
- To teach or instruct them in understanding the ministry.
- To help them identify and clarify the beliefs in their hearts.

The person's part:
- To be willing to seek out and note their issues.
- To be prepared to embrace and accept their beliefs, emotions and memories.

The Holy Spirit's part:
- To guide and inspire the minister and person in the session.
- To reveal God's truth and bring freedom.

Ways that God may communicate with people
An old saying says that *God talks how you listen*. He made your brain and soul exactly how He intended it to be. Some people think in words, others in pictures or impressions; let me offer some of the common ways that God might communicate truth to you.

1. In words:
I tend to think in words, so mostly when God uses my mind to communicate truth to me it comes in words. Interestingly I have noticed that as I have become more and more free that I also receive pictures and impressions at times either for myself or others. Some people get stuck here because they are waiting for flashes of light and a booming voice, or an audible word from outside your body. I explain it this way. My computer is set up with the fonts, letter styles, writing size and so on that I like. If I were to give it to you and ask you to write me a note, when you returned it to me, I might exclaim; *that is just my writing!* That's true; you just used my faculties or equipment to communicate your message to me.

In the ministry room, having identified the heart belief, I simply encourage people to let their minds go. When they hear something, occasionally people might explain that it just seemed like their own thoughts, but they heard this or that. We test and see whether or not it is God by looking at the old belief. Perhaps a person may have always thought that they were dumb. It felt true to them. Now they look for belief and cannot find it, or it is no longer true; it has always been true to them, but it is gone.

2. *Pictures or impressions:*
Many people think in pictures. I remember a man who was suffering from a rejection belief of some kind. When this man spent time with his own children, he would put his face up against their face as a sign of love and affection, indicating acceptance and connection. The man was focusing on his belief and feeling that he was rejected, and God gave him a picture, an impression of the Heavenly Father putting His face against the mans. Needless to say, he was deeply touched and moved. However God communicates to us, it is like a *prophetic now word* applied to our historical event.

In fact, I was ministering to a young man one day and as he embraced the heart belief that he held, the Holy Spirit took some words from a prophetic word that he had received a number of years earlier, and applied it to his belief, bringing healing. Why did it not bring healing before? The young man did not know what he believed in his heart up until this time when we exposed it. Then the Holy Spirit applied the words to the belief.

3. *Scriptures:*
Very often the Holy Spirit will use a scripture that people know well in their minds and apply it to issues in their hearts. By way of example, I was ministering to a lady recently and she was in a memory where she was struggling to keep up with the other children in being able to do her school work. As a result, she had come to a conclusion and belief that she still suffered with daily along the lines of; *I am dumb because I cannot do the schoolwork like the other kids.* As she concentrated on the school memory and felt the belief, the Lord put into her mind the book of Ecclesiastes: *Everything is meaningless!*

For her, this meant that the activity that she was basing her identity on really did not matter. This brought her freedom. If the reference that she was measuring herself against was meaningless then the conclusion that she arrived at had no basis and could not be true either. This was not a conscious act on her part to think differently, it was the result of the truth which the Holy Spirit communicated to her.

4. Realizations:
Several years ago, I ministered to a young man who came with the presenting problem of feeling as though he was responsible for everything that went wrong in his family life, his workplace, and even to some extent the world. As he connected with the feeling, we arrived at the place where he learnt a belief something like; *It's my fault if bad things happen.* As a small boy he was traveling in the back seat of the family car. They had an accident with another car as they entered an intersection. It was an emotionally traumatic event for the little boy. His father whipped around and said sharply, *have you got your seatbelt on?*

Now, it may seem ridiculous, but in that emotionally charged moment the boy thought; *This bad thing is my fault because I haven't gotten my seat belt on!* These thoughts are burned deeply into our brains in moments of crisis through an electro-chemical process known as protein synthesis.

As we explored the memory, he discovered that afterward it turned out that he did in fact have his belt on. He now realized that the truth was that it was not his fault at all. He had believed that it was because, after the moment of shock, it was too late to reinterpret the belief for him as a child after the emotional intensity subsided because the belief was in his heart. But now many years later the Holy Spirit reminded him of the complete picture and set him free.

Personally, I believe that one of the reasons that this ministry is so effective is that God dwells in eternity and not time (Isaiah 57:15). He is everywhere all of the time. He is already there ten years from now, and He is there in your memory, whether you knew of Him or not, as a child. So, we can identify your belief up here in time and counsel you about it with minimal change. But when He speaks into, and helps you reinterpret, your event with His truth He is actually there!

Another example of a realization could be a child coming into a room where mother and father are having a heated argument. In that moment the child believes that it is somehow their fault. Looking back and exploring the memory through the eyes of God they now realize, as they see more of the picture that was not as emotionally intense, that the parents were already fighting before they entered the room. So, how could it be their fault? God will at times bring freedom through realization. I have also seen at times people being set free at the moment where they realize why they believe what they believe, and where it came from, and for them that is the healing.

5. *Sensations, feelings, knowing:*
God is indeed very creative in how He communicates with us. Normally we do not know what He is going to do, or how He will do it. Sometimes He will give us insight into what He is about to say or do. I think in part this is on the job training for words of knowledge and learning to hear his voice for ourselves.

I recall one lady who had suffered severe physical abuse, and as she was accessing memories and beliefs, there was a light coming into the picture. When the light came in, she felt peaceful and calm, safe. I was frantically going through my theology to make sure that this was something Biblical. Remembering, Jesus, light of the world reassured me that this was something that God might do. The bottom line was that her fears were resolved.

Other people report simply feeling love. Still more, report that they just know that the beliefs they held are not true. I remember asking one lady after a session what she now thought of God. She thought about it for a moment, and then replied; *He's clever, He's very clever!* Amen. Our God is indeed very clever.

Wiring
Sometimes God will multitask and use the ministry room as a training ground for you or the recipient. Remember before David went up against Goliath, he found that God was with him in the private place, killing both lion and bear. He honed his skills as a shepherd boy before he was put into public ministry.

God is always about helping people, and He uses our time doing so to learn about Him and His goodness as we see His love, grace and ability to help His children. As we are faithful in little, it is a training ground for other things. Many times, as people hear from God in their healing moment, it becomes obvious for some of them, that God has put in them faculties such as receiving pictures easily. As they learn to understand what God is saying through the pictures and they reach out to Him for what He is communicating to them, they realize that they could reach out for something for others as well. So, ministry times can be a birthing place for prophetic ministries as they not only discover their gifting, but also get free enough and in the truth enough to use them. (That is in part, not having the words from God convoluted through their own soulish heart beliefs.)

Warning
Many ministries have gone off the rails and brought the ministry into disrepute by suggesting how God should communicate with them. For example, I have heard of people suggesting to picture Jesus in the memory. This is a recipe for disaster, licensing potential deception. I have had people report seeing Jesus in their memories perhaps two or three times in 20 years of ministering *Truth Encounters*. Even these were many years ago, and I cannot be sure that they had not been exposed to other ministries who practiced this and, as a consequence, thought that this was what was expected.

My wife has also been ministering this way for perhaps 10 or 12 years and has rarely seen it either. Our work is to simply help the person identify what it is that they believe, and then pass the ministry time over to the Holy Spirit to communicate truth as He sees fit. We are the assistants in the ministry, not the directors.

- You Will Indeed Be Set Free -

CHAPTER 17
Problem areas that you may periodically encounter

Conscious Objections

We have already discussed that some people will simply not want ministry for some reason; they might propose that they are a new creation so there is nothing left to do, and point to the finished work of the cross. If you cannot help them negotiate these conscious objections then you simply acknowledge their free will and choice. They may simply not agree with this form of ministry and either decide to resolve their problems themselves, or feel that another approach is better for them.

We can only teach about the ministry as best we can and testify to what we have seen and heard in terms of the results that we have experienced. Some ministers feel that now that they see the problems for what they are, and know the answer, that they need to push people to go to God for healing. God Himself does not force anyone to do anything; it is not in His nature. We see this in how Jesus dealt with the disciples recognizing their free will and choice.

John 6:66-67 says, " *66 At this point many of his disciples turned away and deserted him. 67 Then Jesus turned to the Twelve and asked, "Are you going to leave, too?"* (NLT).

He could have proclaimed, *hey you guys, you can't go, I have invested a lot of time in you!* Instead, He enquired as to what they willed to do and which course of action that they had decided on.

Suppression

If you suppress something then you restrain, subdue, repress, or hold it back; like a sneeze, a cough or a yawn, at an inappropriate moment. When we are talking about suppressing memories, we are saying that you have chosen to not permit yourself to look at it for some reason. Perhaps it holds guilt, shame, rejection or some other unsavoury emotion in it. So, we restrain it from coming onto the screen of our minds, pushing it back, as a wilful act denying it, and eventually over time, we have repressed it to where we can no longer readily access it. The neural pathway that connected us to the event has gone from a strong four lane highway with street lights to a broken-down potholed dirt track. It is now barely accessible, and we do not want to go to it in any case.

Usually if people have chosen to remember memories no more as an act of their will, then to see those pictures they now have to choose to see them again. They are still there, in storage, it is just that the connection to them has become weak. I have found that often when people now decide to explore those memories for healing that they come back a piece at a time. Just as they faded out as the connection became weak, now as they try to find them the pathway begins to strengthen.

I recall many young ladies who have pushed down abusive memories. When they have chosen to access the memories, they have come back as little snippets and pieces of pictures. As they have been able to accept each piece then another will emerge. Of course, it does not need to be an abusive situation, it could be something along the lines of denying that your father or mother did not love you. As a result, you push the place where you learnt this out of reach.

Dissociation

I have a wrist watch that has written on the back of it, Waterproof to 30 meters. I have often wondered what happens at 31 meters when the pressure becomes too great. Theoretically at least the outside circumstances become too great for it to deal with and it is overwhelmed, crushed, and broken.

Proverbs 18:14, "*A man's spirit sustains him in sickness, but a crushed spirit who can bear?*" (NIV).

Not being able to cope with, or bear a situation, can cause the mind to overload and disconnect from the event. Modern homes often have a circuit breaker on the electrical system in case the wiring is overloaded and damage might occur. If this looks like happening, it simply breaks the connection that allows the power to flow into the situation. Mentally we seem to have the same kind of protection in our wiring. If something is happening to us that we cannot bear, then the mind disconnects or dissociates from what is going on.

Over the years, I have found this to be a common phenomenon with traumas such as sexual abuse. If a twenty-year-old person was being sexually imposed on, in perhaps a rape or coercive sexual encounter, they nowadays, would normally have at least a basic understanding of the sexual act. If the same abuse is played out on, for example, a four-year-old, they have no understanding whatsoever of that which is going on. It is overwhelming and they cannot cope, so they disconnect from the event.

Often, they will project their minds onto some other activity to escape from the situation. After the event, the emotions and memories from the event remain compartmentalized and shut off because of the extreme feelings such as fear and powerlessness that they contain. There is usually some kind of belief objecting to connecting to the contents of the memory. This could be thoughts such as; *if I go there, I will not be able to cope, I will be out of control, I will die,* and so on. These need to be identified and resolved.

Story
A number of years ago, we were doing a school in another state, and there was in attendance, a young married man. From time to time his wife would appear for short periods of time but seemed unwilling to be very involved with the group. We were having a break and the Pastor asked if I would see the young lady and explain about the ministry. I agreed, and not knowing what her issue was, I went through how the *Truth Encounters* ministry worked. She thanked me and left. A little later the Pastor came back and informed me that she wanted ministry but did not have any memories relating to her problem.

Once we began the session, I found that her presenting symptom was that she was unable to have a sexual relationship with her husband because of the feelings that it produced in her. The emotions that she described were consistent with someone who had been abused. As she tried to connect the feelings with a historical event which matched that which she was experiencing, she reported that she had no memories whatsoever. I explained to her that there was some kind of belief that she had that prevented her from seeing what had happened to her, and that it had been an act of her will not to see the memories for that reason. I went on to encourage her that it will also be an act of her will to see why she objected to seeing her memory pictures.

After concentrating for a moment, she announced that it had been a member of family, a close relative who had done it. The perpetrator was considered to be an exemplary Christian and she believed that she could not possibly accept the event because of the closeness of the relative. She further believed that, because of their relationship to the father and mother, she could not tell her parents what had happened. This overload caused her to completely disconnect with the memory altogether. Once this was resolved, she was able to accept that which had happened to her and process the beliefs from the abuse and be healed.

A couple of years ago I was in that town again and she came over and greeted me. She had two small children in her arms and another holding her hand, so I am guessing that the original issue was resolved.

Before our children grew up, and as I would be driving them to school, they would often comment to each other, *Dad's dissociated!* They would see the glazed look and disconnection from the trip to school, as I was thinking in my mind through some ministry case or wrestling with understanding a scripture. The difference is that there was no reason for me to not reconnect with reality. For people who have suffered trauma and disconnected there is a reason.
The ministry in this situation is exactly the same. You just have to have their will aligned, and work through the objection belief before the healing can come. Usually, as with other beliefs, once the beliefs have been taken to heart in an abuse, these beliefs will now be associated with any later abuses and used to qualify these events as well. Other beliefs can of course be added from later times of offence if the circumstances or situation is different.

These memory bubbles, containing a younger version of you, hold reasons made by your will at the time as to why you do not want to see the event. It is valuable to remember that the current version of you is the *executive member of the board* if you like, and holds ultimate sway in exerting and committing your will.

Personas, masks and denial

The Pharisees and teachers of the law adopted a religious image which presented themselves as Holy men who were right with God. Many people who feel that they are not good enough as they are, will adopt some kind of mask or persona that they feel will make them acceptable.

We moved areas a lot when I was going through school, and I had to make new friends and fit into a new town environment many times. One of the ways that I found that made me accepted was to be the *funny guy*. For me this became my mask and you really could not get any deeper than jokes with me.

For some preachers, they don't feel that they are good enough just being themselves, and when they take to the platform you wonder who this new person is that you have not seen before. They are a mixture of their favourite speakers, which they know are accepted! For some people it is difficult at first for them to let you get behind their created image of themselves. You need patience and love to have them trust you sufficiently to take the mask off and own their inadequacies. These images often are not based on truth in regards to who they really are.

Denial and self-justification is also another possible hindrance to helping people receive ministry. If they feel that they have, for example, *every right to be angry!* Often, they will not be prepared to look at what it is in their lives that has been tapped into producing the response. Many people deny that they have any issues at all. It is everyone else that is at fault! As the saying goes; *everyone is messed up except for you and me, and now we mention it, I am not that sure about you!*

Is this counselling?

We do not consider this type of ministry to be counselling. We are not giving instructions regarding efforts that people should undertake to resolve their problems. We simply teach them about what God will do for them if they want to receive from Him. Then, if they choose to connect with the beginnings of their presenting issues, we assist them in defining that which they believe in their hearts. Rather than this being something that they can do, these sessions are all about letting God do what He promised to do in setting them free.

In the event that we do offer them some teaching in a session, we are simply forwarding the advice or counsel that the Bible gives us all. We are not telling them that they have to do this. We are simply helping them see how their lives could function better from a Biblical standpoint. As with all the instruction of scripture, it is entirely our choice as to whether or not we do it. Our work in the ministry room is to help them to receive from God in order for them to be able to live in God's order.

Is this psychology?
Physiology is the biological study of the living organisms of the body. Doctors understand the parts of the body and for the most part understand from these studies how the organs of the body function. They are not wrong about their observations and have some success in treating various maladies, and we are thankful to God for their efforts. We acknowledge of course that only the work of the Holy Spirit can bring miraculous, complete, and many times instant healing.

The New Testament is written in the Koine Greek language, and the word for soul is from the Bible; 'psuche.' In Latin the word for soul is; 'psyche,' which they identify as the identity or personality. Words such as psychology or psychiatry therefore refer to doctors who study and help people with the problems which relate to their souls.

The beginning of these studies historically points back to around 140 years ago. The Bible is the ultimate book explaining the activities of the soul pre-dating man's observations by a considerable amount of time. So, is what we are presenting: a study of the soul? Yes. Personally, I have never read a psychology book and simply began trying to help people by referencing the bible to find out how to do it. I had a break over Christmas in 2017 and the thought came into my mind to examine what they say that the unconscious or subconscious represents, and so I read a couple of internet articles on the subject.

Chapter 17: Problem areas that you may periodically encounter

The prefixes: un = not, and sub = under or below

The articles considered this as thought that is not conscious thought, or thought that is going on under the consciousness. From the various articles that I read, nobody seems to be able to clearly define which is which. In conclusion, what they noted that they are observing is the activities and issues presenting that are largely the same as that which the Bible says about the *heart*. Many of the things that they have learnt about the soul are not wrong; they are just limited without the Holy Spirit in terms of how they can resolve them. Just as with their observations of the body, they are limited with their treatments, so too are these *soul* doctors limited in that which they can offer. We appreciate their efforts and acknowledge that they bring some measure of help. The discovery and development of psychology was heralded as a great move forward for mankind's ability to heal himself, but if they had read a Bible, they would have found that the information in its fullness was there all along.

Very often people have come to us for help after many years of $200 a session visits to a psychologist. Dr. Jesus proceeds to consistently resolve their issues at no cost having already paid the price Himself. I am in no way trying to diminish the efforts or knowledge of these professionals; I am simply saying that God can do what they/we cannot.

Flow chart
The ministry process:
A person comes to you with a problem. This could be a mental, emotional, relational, addictive, spiritual, sexual or physical issue.
↓
They may have been *set off* or *triggered* by a life situation producing for example: anxiety, anger, sadness, bitterness, resentment, guilt, inferiority, rejection and so on.
↓
Your role is to help them focus on these feelings and reactions and to identify the **self**-beliefs which they believe at *heart* level, and which they may no longer immediately consciously access.
↓
The key components that you are trying to connect here are: The emotions, the **self**-beliefs producing the emotions, and the matching

memory pictures. (No pictures prenatal, perhaps a feeling or a sense of something)

↓

You have them focus on the presenting feelings and using questions help them to discover the **self**-beliefs producing the emotion, OR

↓

If they have a **self**-belief, such as, *I just never think that I am good enough*, have them connect with the feeling that should be associated with such a thought. (The emotion often comes up as the story is related or the memory is accessed and described.)

↓

Request that they let memories come to them or wilfully look for the memory picture, if they don't already have it, which contains the thoughts and feelings. (With some pictures that are remembered, it is not always immediately obvious as to why the beliefs have been interpreted here.)

↓

Having refined and identified the belief that was learnt, invite God to bring Truth. (You can be creative in how you request this to avoid being repetitive, but using phrases such as, *Lord, would you like to show Fred how you see this situation? Lord, would you touch Fred by revealing your Truth to replace what he perceives as the truth here? Lord, what would you like Fred to know about the belief that he holds?* and so on.)

Note:
How you address God in this setting is up to you. Some people just say; 'God can you please ...' others might invite Jesus to minister to the person. This is also Biblical as it is the Spirit of Christ who is communicating with them. Someone else might ask the Holy Spirit, or the Spirit of truth to free them with the truth. I often just say 'Lord,' but at times, mix it up a bit. I have never seen God hold back His blessing because we did not get the *method* exactly correct. If you really felt the need to be pernickety and be doctrinally accurate in regards to this, you could offer a prayer such as, *Father, in the name of Jesus, would you please bring your truth to 'Fred' through the Holy Spirit.* (And then seek ministry for your own fear of getting it wrong; cheeky grin!)

— Chapter 17: Problem areas that you may periodically encounter —

I offer this guideline as an example of how a ministry could flow, to help with what you are looking for, where you are looking, and how you look. In practice it all happens quite naturally and organically as you listen to a person's story and ask questions when appropriate. The Holy Spirit really will inspire your thoughts. When you first begin, feeling like you don't know what to do is a common, expected part of stepping into something new. You are beginning with far more information than I had. In the early days I would commence a session with someone, and if we seemed stuck or I did not know how to proceed I would announce that I felt it was a good place to finish for the day. Then I would go and pray and try to work out what I should do next.

- You Will Indeed Be Set Free -

CHAPTER 18
The potential Demonic Element

Introduction
As we begin to discuss the connection between evil spirits and ministering to people, I want to make a couple of points very clear up front.

Firstly, we do not go into a ministry session looking for demons, generational problems or entry points from any other source. If we come from a method, or this is what you do, follow this process type training, we will often gravitate to being directive and pre-empting what the problem might be. I have seen ministries that work through a particular list of demons, or we break this or that as their standard ministry model, and, many times, they see very few or limited results.

We begin with what is your problem? Along the way we may become aware of demonic power being involved. Even when these spirits are discerned, our primary interest is the ground, terrain, activity, or belief that gives them place and not the spirit itself. The devil and His demons are completely and utterly totally defeated and there is no other way to regard him.

We can accurately say then, that for a believer, the devil is not the problem, rather it is the area of our thinking or inner believing that gives him ground and deceives us into moving our will to participate with him. So, we really are not demon focused, instead we are targeting the presenting problem that a person carries, being aware that *at times* it *might be* empowered, amplified or locked in by an evil spirit. Our mission, in co labouring to set the captives free, is to resolve wrong believing and areas of deception working under the ministry of the Spirit of Truth.

Examining beliefs at a heart level is the quickest way that I have seen to expose the ground held by many evil spirits. The beliefs themselves may be the ground for the demons, or the resultant sin choices and behaviour may give them place.

The strong man's goods

A number of years ago I was pulling down an old house on our property in order to build a new one on the site. In the meantime, we had a large shed and I set up my office and a lounge room in there. There was also a lot of furniture stacked in there. While I was working outside some of the children came out screaming that there was a snake in the building. Now I could have taken the attitude that I would just deal with it if it showed up. However, I felt that it was my duty and responsibility to find where it had come in and seal that off and then expose it and deal with it so that it could not cause harm.

As I have said, if we become aware that a *demon* is in the house, we have a duty to those that we are responsible for to find out where it came from and evict it as soon as possible. Sometimes when I go camping, there will be a mosquito in the tent. I will not rest until I have tracked that thing down and eliminated it before I try to sleep. I know that in the night with its buzzing, it will rob my peace and ruin my functionality and mood for the following day. Consequently, it is prudent for me to deal with it as soon as possible. First, as with the snake I have to expose where it is hiding and block up the place where it has come in!

Exposing the enemy through teaching

It has been proposed that fully one third of Jesus' recorded ministry to people in the gospels was dealing with demons in some way. We know that before He ministered, He often taught the people. A number of years ago we were ministering in a large church in the Pacific and immediately prior to lunch I had taught on rejection. There was a young lady who brought the meal to us at the Pastors house, and as she put the food in front of us, I noticed that she had tears in her eyes. I commented to her; *The rejection teaching touched you didn't it?* She responded that it did. I asked her if she wanted me to pray for her and she indicated that she did. Across the table I took authority over the spirit of rejection and commanded it to go in the name of Jesus. She had a manifestation and I asked her if it had gone. She informed me that it had and so we proceeded to eat our lunch. The point is that this was easily done because she saw her problem. If the setting had been right, *Truth Encounters* would have been a good option for further healing. If she had not understood the source of her issue and the spiritual element of her problem, most probably nothing would have happened.

In the mid-1990s an intellectual lady came for some ministry advice. As she described her problem it became evident to me that she was also carrying a spirit of rejection. I explained this to her and how it worked but she was struggling with the concept, and so thanked me and left. Several months later she returned and confirmed that she now believed that what I had explained was true. Now that she had seen the spiritual element of her problem it was only a matter of moments and she was free. She later reported that she was now able to get on with people whom she formerly struggled with and generally felt better.

I want to make the point that if I had tried to cast out the spirit without her having a realization that it was present, I would have been wasting my time. God will not necessarily set her free because I want her to be free. He will set her free when, by her own will, she wants Him to free her, which will normally require her understanding her need. If this were not the case then God would automatically set everyone free of everything without the consent of their free will and choice. Even the demoniac in Mark chapter 5 came to Jesus and fell down before Him. Jesus often said things such as; *do you want to be made well?* (John 5:6).

Another factor that I would like to mention regarding this lady's ministry was that at that time we did not minister *Truth Encounters* and although she reported improvement and that the power had gone out of her rejection she was still not completely whole in that area. A few years later she returned for further ministry in which the *truth made her completely free.*

What are the strong man's goods?
A strong man's *goods* or *possessions* are those things which he holds that strengthen his position. The Greek word translated as *goods* or *possessions* is *huparchonta*, which also means *that which one has* or *his property.*

Luke 11:20-21, " [20] *But if I drive out demons by the finger of God, then the kingdom of God has come to you.* [21] *"When a strong man, fully armed, guards his own house, his possessions are safe"* (NIV, Emphasis mine).

Let me suggest that he is fully armed with areas of deception that protect those areas that he considers his property, possessions or goods. These possessions that give him *a place* are the beliefs that we hold that cause us to serve him and participate with him. For example:

- A spirit of bitterness will hold hurts and beliefs resulting from being hurt or abused.
- A spirit of rebellion will hold beliefs relating to injustice.
- A spirit of pride will hold beliefs relating to inferiority.
- A spirit of self-pity will hold beliefs to do with nobody caring about the host and so on.
- The one who is stronger is the Spirit of truth, because truth overpowers the power of deception just as light dispels darkness.
- So is the spirit the problem or, is the property or possessions that he holds that give him a place, the issue?

Ephesians 4:27, *"... nor give **place** to the devil"* (NKJV, Emphasis mine).

Ephesians 4:27, *"... and do not give the devil **a foothold**"* (NIV, Emphasis mine).

Giving the devil a foothold or a place to stand, through what we believe and the resultant way that we act, is the true nature of the problem. Again, we look to the original Greek language and see that *foothold* and *place* come from the word *topos* which means a location, a home, or even an opportunity. So often through what we believe we consciously or unconsciously yield a portion of our personality, soul or body for the demon to stand on.

Being *fully armed* relates to his ability to protect his position. For example, if his possessions which give him place are beliefs relating to inferiority then his ability to defend those beliefs are the pride response that comes from those beliefs. Now he is safe because the host will not go to anyone for help because their pride will not allow them to be *under* another person. Remember this is because the solution to inferiority that the devil suggests is to make you *over* or *above* everyone else in pride. This means that you believe that you know more or better and have more wisdom than anyone else. If we continue to use the same examples the *fully armed* component of injustice beliefs is the rebellion reaction. Now the person is captive because they cannot submit to another.

In the case of a control spirit, the person's insecurity is the issue. To trust another would mean that they are no longer in control, and this is the defence of the strongman and so on. This is why ministering to the root heart belief, rather than trying to cast out the demon by attacking his defences is a far more effective and permanent way of dealing with the spirit. He is now weak and easy to cast out because he has lost his *possessions* which gave him a *place* and so this is also a gentler approach for the person.

Many times, the spirit is attached to sinful behaviour, attitudes, reactions and responses that are retaliatory by nature. The name of the demon is the name of ungodly sinful activities such as unforgiveness, resentment, bitterness, ungodly control, rebellion, pride, hatred, self-rejection, fear of rejection and so on. I need to point out that all of these can and do exist without the presence of a demon inside the host. Either way the beliefs need to be dealt with to remove the areas that the devil can work through from outside, or that are strongholds of evil spirits on the inside.

Two of the main ways that the demons have a place then, is firstly by holding people captive to pain and hurt coming from heart beliefs. Secondly, they are from responses that you believe will resolve the issues proceeding from these beliefs. This could, along with the emotional reactions that we have described, include things such as lustful or immoral activities, violence, addictive behaviour, theft, lying, criticism, and so on.

How right was Louis Pasteur when he made an observation relating to the destructive power of the unseen enemy that we now know as germs! *The germ is nothing, the terrain is everything!* In a spiritual sense we could replicate this principle by saying that the demon is nothing, the environment or beliefs that give him place are everything. The only hold he has on us to use us, manipulate us, and keep us in bondage is some area of deception or wrong believing in the mind, heart, or both. The *germ is nothing* and consequently our focus is not on him, he simply *flags* the real problem. Once we know the type of root belief and likely circumstance that it was learnt in, we can deal with the terrain.

The 'dung' god
Jesus described Satan as *Beelzebub* which means the *dung god*, or *the lord of the flies*. This gives us a great perspective on how God

regards demons. They are nothing, they are just like flies. The only power that they have is whatever you are deceived into giving them, which is why when you know the truth it will set you free. I think that most of us who started out with a *cast out the demons* focus, and neglected healing the broken hearts, would agree with me that many times we would shoo away the flies on Monday only to find that we had to do it again a week later. Some people would stay free, or have a measure of deliverance but many, even though they may have had powerful deliverances and manifestations, would return bound again.

Whereas when we take the *Truth Encounters* model, we see them completely free in the area ministered to, and are often not even aware if there was a demon there or not because we took his goods in which he trusted in. It is much gentler for the person than attacking a fully armed spirit if we remove that which he trusts in. In short, clean up the dung and there is no further reason for the flies to be there. They need food and the dung heap as their place. The fly is nothing; the dung is *everything*!

Swept and empty

When Jesus used the picture of that which the spirit considers to be *his house, or place that he inhabits* He states that if this abode, which is based on the possessions of the demon is left empty, then it is likely that the evil spirit will return. Why is this?

Let me propose that the property of the demon that gave him place was the deceptive beliefs that the host or person held. So, if the house is left empty and not filled with God's truth through the ministry of the Spirit of truth, then there is nothing stopping him from returning. If knowing the Truth will set you free, and if this is done by the Spirit of Christ, then you will remain free indeed.

Matthew 12:43-44, "*43 When an unclean spirit goes out of a man, he goes through dry places, seeking rest, and finds none. 44 "Then he says, 'I will return to my house from which I came.' And when he comes, he finds it empty, swept, and put in order*" (NKJV).

Repentance and deliverance

Once a spirit has established a strong hold on your hurts or sinful reactions, he is going to replay them as inner thinking or addictive and often repetitive behaviour. He is also going to amplify your responses and the intensity of emotion that you hold. People with demonic powered beliefs may often not be able to control their feelings and have an inordinate response in how they react to stressors.

When we talk about repentance, people normally consider it to mean to turn from your sin. This turning is actually a by-product of repentance. The word translated as *repent* from the original Greek language is *Metanoeo* and it means to *think differently* or *reconsider*, or *to change one's mind*. When we think differently about what we are doing, reconsider our ways and then change our minds, the by-product will be turning from sin. In the first instance we need to know that our thinking and resultant deeds are wrong in the first place, and we do this through learning the ways of God from His word. In the epistle 1 John and chapter 3 we see that Jesus came to destroy the works of the devil.

1 John 3:8, *"He who sins is of the devil, for the devil has sinned from the beginning. For this purpose the Son of God was manifested, that He might destroy the works of the devil"* (NKJV).

Having established that Jesus came to destroy the works of the devil that were operating in and through mankind, we now observe that He came preaching; *repent for the Kingdom of heaven is at hand*. Why?

He did this because in order to destroy the devil's works in us, he needs us to stop cooperating with our enemy by our own will and volition. He needs for us to think differently, reconsider our ways and change our minds to living the ways of the Kingdom of God. We do this by renewing our minds and then deciding that we want to be hearers and doers of the word. But as we have described in an earlier chapter the Apostle Paul had set himself in this stance as he outlined in Romans chapter 7, but was unable to do that which he had decided to do with his conscious mind. He needed a change of thinking at heart level as well before he could be fully repentant, and this is a gift of God through healing ministries such as *Truth Encounters* and deliverance.

2 Timothy 2:24-26, " ²⁴ *And the servant of the Lord must not strive; but be gentle unto all men, apt to teach, patient,* ²⁵ *In meekness instructing those that **oppose themselves**; if God peradventure will give them **repentance to the acknowledging of the truth**;* ²⁶ *And that they may recover themselves out of the snare of the devil, who are **taken captive by him** at his will"* (KJV, Emphasis mine).

As in the case of Paul, these people oppose themselves because how they want to act with their minds is not in agreement with how they do actually act, which is based on the deceptive beliefs that they hold in their hearts. The final result is that they remain in bondage to the devil acting out his will and manifesting his nature. They are doing this even though they are believers, in part because they believe that their actions are *just what they want to do,* and are not aware of the devil's involvement. In 2 Timothy chapter 2 and verse 25 it refers to the change of thinking or repentance coming as a result of acknowledging *the truth.*

Our mission is to gently instruct them and teach them the truth about the roots of their issues and how they can receive freedom from captivity. Mostly evil spirits have a place in us through something that we believe either consciously or unconsciously. This could include not believing that a part of the problem is a demon.

Spiritual 'armour'
Whilst we are mainly focused on the issue, or the 'dung', it is good to be aware of the possibilities of spiritual interference, which is why I am writing this whole section.

Story
At one time a lady travelled a long way to receive *Truth Encounters* ministry. Before we began the ministry session, and following a prompt, I prayed for her and she received the baptism in the Holy Spirit as evidenced by her speaking in other tongues. As we proceeded to go through her memories, we identified the beliefs in her heart, as we normally would, and God communicated things to her that were consistent with what would normally happen.

Chapter 18: The potential Demonic Element

This is the only time that I have ever seen this, but at the end of the session she reported that all of her problems were the same and that her new Holy Spirit tongue seemed ridiculous to her. Again, I felt prompted to ask if I could pray for her against a spirit before she left and she responded that this would be alright with her. I took authority over a spirit of doubt and unbelief and commanded it to leave and come off her mind and emotions. Nothing obvious happened.

A couple of days later she was booked to come in for another session before she made the long journey home. I was not particularly looking forward to this time together because all that we usually saw God free people through did not seem to have had much effect on her. When she arrived, she alighted from her vehicle beaming and reported that she was all healed and loved her new prayer language. The spirit of doubt and unbelief had been blocking her from receiving any of the things that had happened in her prayer session. Once the spirit was gone, she had a download and was completely set free. Following is an excerpt from the testimony that she emailed to me a week later;

"Steve and Em, wow you would not believe the changes in me!! But then of course you do believe!! Praise the Lord...here we go...just overflowing with the Holy Spirit like the incredible hulk, just wants to burst out, the heaviness, anxiety, confusion, sadness, back pain, sleeplessness...all gone, zapped, now light, joyous, calm, strengthened."

And so, it went on, including no longer needing her medication for a physical problem. The point is that, if we were not aware of the possibility of a spirit or spirits being involved, it is unlikely that she would have received her healing.

Story
On another occasion I was ministering to a young lady who had suffered considerable sexual abuse. God was faithfully setting her free from the beliefs that she held from the painful memories. As the Lord resolved one particular memory, she reported joy and peace in regards to her new freedom. She asked me a question not relating to emotion from the event. In this instance she had been sodomized and her question was in regards to whether or not I thought this could have been implicated in a problem with moving

her bowels. I shot up a quick thank you prayer as I had missed it, and could have left her with this problem for life.

I related to her that there may well be a spirit of infirmity that attached to her as a result of the ungodly act towards her. At this point some of you may be thinking why should she get a spirit when she did not do anything wrong? This is a reasonable question so let me briefly digress.

If you went to your neighbours' house and they hit you over the head with a piece of wood, who sinned? They did. Who has the lump on the forehead? You do. Sin creates an opening just as when parents deeply or repetitively reject their children, and the child receives a corresponding spirit. It would be rare for a person to ask for or want a demon; something has happened to them, usually that they did not ask for.

In the case of this young lady, she was a victim of an ungodly sexual bond and along with the emotional trauma this created an entry point for the spirit. I will explain this more fully under the heading *integrity*. I simply addressed the spirit of infirmity that had come in through the lustful activity and told it to go. She looked a little bit uncomfortable for a moment and then told me that it had gone. A few days later I received a phone call from her and she reported that her system was now working perfectly. Again, if we were not aware of the possibilities of a spirit operating, she could have gone on through life with the problem.

A lady once came to me after a meeting where I had spoken and ministered in their church. She asked for some wisdom for a lady that she was looking after who was bitter and angry against God because her husband had died. I suggested that she tell the lady that; *God does not always get what He wants*. He does not want wars, children abused or people saying nasty things to each other. He has in some sense limited Himself in evidently giving all of His creation free will and choice. He is not pleased, and eventually will judge using the Word of God to measure. Even for believers He in some measure has limited His activities to faith which is based on how we see His character.

CHAPTER 19
Names of demons and touching the spirit realm

Some people feel that they need to know the names of all the demons and get them right before they will leave. You can simply say something such as; *you spirit that is attached to this or that, leave in the name of Jesus.* There are books around with pages of lists of the names of demons. At one time I remember reading a book with one of these lists and thinking how will I remember the names of all these evil spirits? A scripture that I had read came to remembrance in my mind about the *lying spirits* in 1 Kings 22:22. In this passage the prophets were looking to say what the Kings wanted to hear in order to receive their acceptance and favour. The usual reason that people tell lies is a fear of rejection and it is the most common reason that I have found that causes people to lie.

I have dealt with a number of people where this has become a demonic problem and they simply cannot tell the truth even when they want to. The basis of freedom in these people in the first instance came with resolving the rejection beliefs, but I digress.

In the case of the prophets wanting to please the Kings and say what they wanted to hear, this opened them to having a spirit attached to them.

1 Kings 22:21-23, " *²¹ Then a spirit came forward and stood before the LORD, and said, 'I will persuade him.' ²² "The LORD said to him, 'In what way?' So he said, 'I will go out and be a lying spirit in the mouth of all his prophets.' And the LORD said, 'You shall persuade him, and also prevail. Go out and do so.' ²³ "Therefore look! The LORD has put a lying spirit in the mouth of all these prophets of yours, and the LORD has declared disaster against you"* (NKJV).

What I learnt from studying and meditating on the passage is that the spirit was not a *lying spirit*, it was just a generic nondescript spirit. It was only able to attach itself to that which was yielded to sin, in this case lying. It could not go and be a spirit of lust or bitterness because that was not the area of the personality or body that was being made available to sin. So, the name of a spirit is simply the area of the person that they hold. If it's bitterness, its bitterness, lust, lust, lying, lying and so on. It exists there because it has access to the person in some way, often through their unwitting yielded ness in following sinful behaviour, attitudes and responses.

Many in the church seem to have this idea that the devil already has spirits with special names, functions and job descriptions in stock that he can send at will to attack people. You can almost imagine how some might think this would look in the spirit world; *We are running low on spirits of bitterness in New York, could you send 5,000 more please? And we need another 10,000 spirits of lust to drive the porn industry in London!* In all probability a spirit that may have previously functioned as bitterness because of the participation of its last host, could well have a role of insanity or mental illness in the next person that they are able to inhabit.

When they run through generation lines, they seem to be able to promote the same beliefs and ground to operate on that was in previous generations. As a result, you may see issues such as ungodly control, lust, unforgiveness or rejection run through families, with corresponding physical maladies, until someone receives freedom from Christ Jesus.

Touching the spirit realm
When I was a young man, we used to go camping in canvas tents. This material was excellent at keeping out the rain and weather. The only problem that it had was that to some extent the material seemed to soak up the water to the point of saturation as a part of its ability to have the rain runoff. So, if you touched the material anywhere when it was raining that was now a place where it leaked. The spirit realm is very much like this. We are always surrounded by spiritual elements and wherever we touch it, that is where we have given it access to leak into our environment.

Let me suggest some areas where we may create openings, and if there is demonization that goes with it then the following list of examples could all be the names of demons. We could address them as; *you spirit that has been involved in holding Fred into 'rebellious' behaviour.* (This assumes that we have dealt with the injustice beliefs already or concurrently.)

These are some sample areas of the human person that spirits may influence or affect:

- Emotional breaches; fear, bitterness, rejection, inferiority. Etc.
- Mental problems; doubt, unbelief, fantasy, withdrawal, insanity. Etc.
- Moral issues; pornography, fornication, adultery, lying, theft. Etc.
- Relational disharmony; mockery, criticism, judgment, religion. Etc.
- Spiritual alliances; the occult, false religion, witchcraft. Etc.
- Physical bondage; addictions, lusts, altered states, violence, infirmity. Etc.

These are all potential areas of exposure to the spirit realm if we touch it or there is an opening through which it can enter. You will note that virtually all of these are tied to thoughts coming from beliefs, which precipitate and present in decisions. This should re centre us on the need for truth at every level of our being so that we can make good protective choices.

Integrity
Most probably when you hear the word integrity you think of a business man or similar who conducts their dealings in an upright and trustworthy manner. The word integrity actually means; the state of being entire, or whole. As an example, if you could imagine your skin as a God given barrier to protect you from the elements as well as various bacteria and diseases. While my skin holds its unbroken integrity and remains whole you could pour, for example, hepatic B virus over my arm and I would not be harmed. But if you created a small cut or opening in the wholeness of my skin then I would become infected and get sick.

We have already mentioned that the word for being saved is sozo and that a part of the meaning of that word includes to deliver or protect and coming to wholeness. The more whole we are in regards to truth about God, ourselves, how to deal with others, and the spiritual world that we have, the more delivered we are. This is our best protection against possible infection from the spiritual realm and this is why children are the most vulnerable, because they have the least amount of truth and understanding. They need our spiritual protection and instruction to bring them up in the counsel of the Lord.

When we have a break or breach in our spiritual or emotional integrity, it is a potential entry point for a spirit. This could be a time of fear or trauma. It could be a time of abuse where our understanding of the situation is overwhelmed and we are out of control. It could also be at a time where we are on drugs or drunk, and our normal resistance and mental integrity is weakened and now we do something sinful that we would not normally do.

I want to reiterate that, the belief that matches the emotional breach is often the entry point for a demon stronghold. Dealing with the beliefs that give ground to the spirit is far more important than the spirit itself.

FINALLY

Finally

I write this book in the hope that the body of Christ will be further equipped to not only speak of the good news but to be the good news. There are many who need to be touched by God through believers walking in the Spirit who know how to help. In this, we, as did Jesus, prove God and His word to be true and uphold His integrity.

John 15:7-9, "*7 If you remain in me and my words remain in you, ask whatever you wish, and it will be given you. 8 This is to my Father's glory, that you bear much fruit, showing yourselves to be my disciples.*" *9 "As the Father has loved me, so have I loved you. Now remain in my love"* (NIV).

In all of our efforts we take comfort that our Lord will guide the whole process. I love Psalm 23 which details that we will walk through this hostile environment called Earth, but have the Lords guidance and the promise of restoration for our souls. Verse five encourages us that even in the presence of our enemies He has promised to take us out to lunch!

Psalm 23:1-6, "*1 The LORD is my shepherd; I shall not want. 2 He makes me to lie down in green pastures; He leads me beside the still waters. 3 He restores my soul; He leads me in the paths of righteousness For His name's sake 4 Yea, though I walk through the valley of the shadow of death, I will fear no evil; For You are with me; Your rod and Your staff, they comfort me. 5 **You prepare a table before me in the presence of my enemies**; You anoint my head with oil; My cup runs over. 6 Surely goodness and mercy shall follow me All the days of my life; And I will dwell in the house of the LORD Forever.*" *(NKJV, Emphasis mine).*

Appendix 1
418Centre details and statement of faith

418Centre is founded on Luke 4:18, and is a training ministry purposed to equip and resource the saints with practical help to present and administer the gospel. Materials will be uploaded as the site continues to develop. The **School of Freedom and Healing** is the main training outreach which is run across the world in different formats tailored to the environment.

You can reach us via the website through the contact page
www.418centre.org

Disclaimer
It is not my purpose to validate every statistic quoted in this publication. As with any studies conducted the results are varied. These references are merely to indicate or illustrate typical data centred around the topics covered.

Note: Truth Encounters Flow Charts on PowerPoint slides are available on the 418centre website.

Truth Encounters Faith Statements
Position of faith:
"We firmly believe that the Bible says what it means and means what it says. Consequently, we believe in, and experience miracles and physical healing, and understand them as being for today. We also believe in healing for the broken hearted, and freedom for captives from various kinds of bondages. We further believe that the gifts of the Spirit are for all of time. Indeed, according to Jesus' promise this is the Holy Spirits era or dispensation, and we are in a better place for His presence and ministry."
JN 14:16   14:26   16:7

Possible differences from other similar ministries:
1. We believe in and practice the gifts of the Holy Spirit in the ministry setting. We acknowledge His work, leading and participation in inspiring our questions and calling to remembrance things learnt from past sessions or training. At times, even showing us what the people coming for ministry may believe. As the Spirit of truth, He is the one who communicates God's truth to the person coming

for help. All of this is in a naturally supernatural manner as we are joined with Him and are one with Him in Spirit.

1 COR 6:17 (Note: people may be being inspired by the Holy Spirit and not be aware that it is Him. They may consider it to be their own thoughts and knowledge…which obviously can also be the case.)
2. We do not necessarily always wait for the person to discover what they believe. Our position is that they have come to us to help them identify what they believe, so if we can FastTrack the process by landing them on or close to what they believe, then we have no problem in doing so. For example, a person comes for ministry and they are obviously agitated and nervous about being able to do the ministry. We have no hesitation in floating one or more possibilities. E.G.s

"Are you by any chance afraid of not being able to do this ministry session?" If the answer is affirmative, this could be followed by questions such as:
"Would it make you a failure if you could not do it?"
"Are you anxious because I might disapprove of you if you can't do it?" Etc. Etc.

People know what they believe and are quick to say things like:
"No, it is more like…. this or that."

We do not hesitate to do this for a number of reasons.
A. It can turn a 50min or more session into a 5min session giving you time to do other things.
B. If you see something and don't present it, you may either miss dealing with that problem or take longer to do other things because their fear of failure or other belief may create a blockage.
C. Sometimes people don't understand what types of beliefs that you are looking for. Suggestions can greatly help them in this. Your own sense of what you are dealing with will increase with experience.

3. Our understanding, experience and theology of the nature and activity of demons may differ considerably from others doing this type of ministry.

4. We may pray for and believe for physical healing in a ministry session, or include Biblical advice in a ministry time flowing in with the truth encounters.

5. We **never** ask people to visualize anything or put 'Jesus,' 'Angels' or any other persons in the memories. In a small percentage of cases people may report seeing these things. We acknowledge that our job is simply to help them identify and connect with what they believe. How the Holy Spirit communicates truth or frees the person is His ministry alone.

Where did 'Truth Encounters' as a term come from?
We first heard the expression 'Truth Encounters' used by Pastor Mike Connell from New Zealand at a conference. His reference to it was relating to a way that God brings freedom through truth to captives. JN 8:32
It was such a good way to describe the ministry that we were doing, that we adopted it as an identifying term.

Note: Ps. Mike may be using an entirely different model to arrive at the same outcomes.

Appendix 2
Other Resources from 418Centre

1. YOU WILL INDEED BE SET FREE
This book explains the basis of how to be healed and set free through a 'Truth Encounter'.

2. HEALING AND FREEDOM THROUGH TRUTH ENCOUNTERS
This detailed publication includes the contents of *YOU WILL INDEED BE SET FREE*, along with considerable other information to help those wishing to minister or gain further understanding.

3. SCHOOL OF HEALING AND FREEDOM Comprehensive Training Manual
This Manual contains all of the materials contained in the books in a study format, as well as other Units relating to bringing freedom, healing and wholeness.

4. SCHOOL OF HEALING AND FREEDOM Basic Seminar Manual
This is the simplified version of the manual for those attending Schools or seminars.

5. PREPARING FOR A 'TRUTH ENCOUNTER'
This booklet is designed as a handout to help position those coming for a 'Truth Encounters' ministry session to understand and receive their breakthrough.

All resources can be purchased via:
U.K purchases, Amazon UK
U.S. purchases, Amazon U.S.A.
Australia purchases, Koorong in Australia, & Amazon Australia.
Africa purchases, CLC booklink Kenya, Jumia, Amazon Africa

Further details about 418Centre can be found on our website:
www.418centre.org

www.ingramcontent.com/pod-product-compliance
Lightning Source LLC
Chambersburg PA
CBHW071928290426
44110CB00013B/1524